C000312144

Spirit
Writer

Spiritwriterspeaks

By
Wendy Sheffield

Grosvenor House
Publishing Limited

This book is published by
Grosvenor House Publishing Ltd
Link House
140 The Broadway, Tolworth, Surrey, KT6 7HT.
www.grosvenorhousepublishing.co.uk

A CIP record for this book
is available from the British Library

ISBN 978-1-80381-203-8
eBook ISBN 978-1-80381-204-5

Acknowledgments

I would like to acknowledge various people who have had an impact on my spiritual life:

To my parents in spirit, who have given me the means to carry on with my spiritual work.

To my son, Alexander Peter Lewis, who had to live through difficult times whilst I was unfolding.

To my Spirit Guide Inspirer (Barnabas) who inspires me every day. He has taught me the true meaning of love.

To all my friends at Sutton Coldfield Spiritualist Church, including Jean Kelford and Chris Beech (International Mediums).

To all my friends at Erdington Christian Spiritualist Church, including Linda Wilson, Rachel Daniels and Lisa Twinks West.

To all my friends at Arthur Findlay College, including Suzanne Gibson-Foy and Penny Hayward, who provide excellent training courses, spiritual assessments and evidential readings.

The Leslie Flint Trust who kindly let me use the transcript of the recording of Harry Price through the mediumship of Leslie Flint (deceased).

Preface

I started my journey as an ordinary lady who spent her life dreaming of being a psychic medium only to discover, after a lifetime's worth of strange occurrences and spirit messages, that I was one – not just any psychic medium, but one that could spirit write using a keyboard!

I hope that by following my journey you too will consider your spiritual side of life. You might recognise gut feelings that often come true, or you might hear inner voices that you are scared to share with the world in case you might be mocked. It was feelings like this that made me believe in myself and discover my true spiritual path, which is to understand my own unfoldment so that I could help others with theirs.

With the aid of my newfound mediumistic ability, I was able to unravel a family mystery going back generations which had caused disharmony amongst them.

In the beginning, I thought I was just imagining what I had heard, but as my life progressed, I started to believe and accept my spiritual journey. It did, however, take a great deal of evidence for me to believe the spirit messages that I was receiving, which included visiting several world class mediums to check my messages. Much to my surprise, everything in these readings confirmed what spirit had told me! I have provided two chapters where I consider the evidence that I have of strange occurrences and predictions that I experienced along my journey.

It was only when I stood up to the outside world about my beliefs that I discovered my true spiritual journey. I now invite you to discover your journey!

My motto is 'believe and you will achieve' which basically means if you believe in yourself, you will gain the confidence to achieve whatever your heart desires!

Wendy Sheffield

Contents

1

What is spirit writing?

Although spirit writing is part of my life now, I thought it important to start with a description of the same to aid understanding. The traditional method of spirit writing is by using a pen and paper. The medium keeps an open mind whilst holding the pen and permits spirit to control her hand, allowing spirit to attempt to write messages which can later be deciphered. This is not to be confused by a 'ghost writer', who voluntarily writes on behalf of someone else on the Earth plane.

When trying to spirit write yourself, it is important to be comfortable and to clear your mind and not to worry about anything. Some people find that music can help them relax. Many automatic writers find that music with vocals can influence their writing, so be cautious in your choice of background tunes. It is important to ground yourself and clear your brain of thoughts and put your pen to paper. Your wrist should be limp whilst you are holding your pen, you are trying to encourage spirit to work through you. Just write the first thing that comes to mind and then keep going. As words pop into your brain, allow your hand to freely write without thinking about what you are writing.

Don't worry about trying to interpret what you have written just yet, figuring out the meaning is something to do when you're all finished. Some people find that asking a specific question is a good way to get the flow started. You can simply write the question on your paper and then see what sort of responses come out. If the answers you're writing don't seem to correspond to your question, don't worry, write them anyway. Often, we get answers to the questions we *didn't* ask. Keep going until it seems like the words have stopped. For some people this can be after ten minutes, for others it can be an hour. Some people like to use a timer, so they don't find themselves sitting at a table all afternoon scribbling things out. After you've finished, it's time to review what you have written. Look for patterns, words, themes that resonate with you. For instance, if you see repeated references to work or jobs, it's possible you need to focus on matters relating to your employment. Watch for names. If you see names you don't recognize, it's possible that you are taking a message for someone else. You may even find pictures such as doodles, characters, or symbols, etc. Keep in mind that your results may be neat and orderly, or they may be chaotic and all over the place. It is important, as with all forms of psychic divination, to practice automatic writing, the more you'll come to understand the messages you are receiving from the other side.

When I first became aware of my spirit writing, spirit tried to work through me using the traditional method of pen and paper. When spirit became aware that I was struggling to keep up with this, they then encouraged me to spirit write using a keyboard – a skill which they knew I had the whole of my life. This, therefore, allowed me to keep up with the spirit communication in a way with which I was familiar.

It took a while before I realised that spirit was trying to communicate through me in this way, but when I learned to exercise control, my messages flowed freely, and I am now able to use this skill to discover new directions for my life as well as guiding other people with their lives, which I love to do!

Spirit will constantly try to communicate with you, which means that you do have to be extremely vigilant in what messages you are receiving in your mind and what is happening to your body. It was by being vigilant with how spirit was working with me that I realised they were using my skill as a fast typist. It is with this newfound skill that I finally discovered a way in which I could finally communicate with the world!

2

Spiritual unfoldment

I will now provide an explanation of 'What is spiritual unfoldment?'. The aim of my book is to help people consider the many ways in which spirit can work with you to help you understand your journey. You may at times feel scared of experiences that you may have, but it is important to remember that this is your fear with which you need to overcome, spirit will not harm you!

Spirit works with people in many ways, so you need to be vigilant and pay attention to any messages spirit sends you. Remember, spirit knows you better than you know yourself and they will, if you let them, encourage you to use any abilities that you have to help others. Personally, I recognised when spirit started to use my ability as a keyboard operator to communicate spirit messages as they knew I was having problems using the traditional pen and paper method. I must add, however, that it took many years for me to able to use my spirit writing effectively, but all my effort has been repaid many times over!

Spiritual unfoldment helps you to understand your spiritual existence and helps you realise who you are and what your personal journey is. It is when you become spiritually aware and begin to communicate and connect to spirit and your guides that they will then be able to guide you in your everyday life.

The first step to unfoldment is to recognise that there is a 'higher self' which you want to know more about. Your interest in spirit will then allow them to assist you on your journey. They will not be able to help you with your life unless you give them permission to do so, however. We will now consider other people's opinions on unfoldment:

Eckhart, T (2020) He was educated at the Universities of London and Cambridge, and he regularly gives his opinion on what he believes is happening around the world on YouTube. He talks about his life journey of self-discovery which started at the age of 29 where he began a profound inner transformation that radically changed the course of his life. He invites people to start their path towards awakening to find who they truly are by considering his journey. He claims that "awakening to happiness" is happening to many individuals around the world which is drawing them to spiritual teachings as it is their awakening. He talks about how it is important to understand who you are and asks you consider how the world sees you now and in the future.

Arthur Findlay College (2018) We will now consider the views of two of Arthur Findlay College mediums who, in one of their workshops, also considered why 'unfoldment' or 'awakening' is taking place. They suggest that there is obviously something much bigger going on in the world due to the increasing need of people seeking guidance from psychics and mediums rather than using traditional methods for guidance.

They have come to this conclusion from listening to many people who have come to them for readings. They suggest that something has awakened within us, or something has happened so that we are made aware of spirit around us and because of this we get an awakening and "get the bug". Because of this awakening, we become aware of our own spirit and consequently spirit is attracted to us to provide encouragement, making you feel like you are "piggy in the middle". Once you feel this way, you believe you have a sense of why you are doing something, what motivates you and what is your inner drive.

They also talk about what is happening in the world today and why people are looking for answers now. They suggest that many people are searching online hoping to find the answer to what life is all about. They suggest that spirit wants to help mankind to teach people about the eternity of life. They suggest that spirit wants to make us aware of the spirit within us. They suggest that spirit wants to remove limitations and wants to expand our understanding, and from this you realise that there is a bigger plan unfolding. They suggest that spirit, despite wanting to help us, are not there to gratify us. If spirit do not come through, you should consider whether you are using the right medium or whether it might not be time to come through for that spirit. Another reason why certain spirits do not come through is because someone else needs to come through with a higher priority. Spirit wants to help us to understand that we are not "mortal"' human beings, and they want to lead us to God. Spiritualism is a now a recognised religion in the UK and spirit will lead us to divine power.

After considering these two accounts, clearly more people are searching for guidance from mediums and psychics to help with their lives because they are not getting answers from traditional methods. With the aid of the internet, people are now able to search for answers in a way in which they were never able to before. This is exactly what happened to me when I was seeking guidance to solve issues within my life. I felt I had no-one to turn to help me understand what I was experiencing. Everyone that I spoke to before I discovered spiritualist churches were all telling me that everything was 'all in my mind' and I just would not accept this as I felt deep down that my experiences were 'real'.

On my journey, I did not find it easy to find spiritual guidance and used to have countless readings from mediums when at times I could not really afford to do so. I desperately wanted answers, and I would listen to anybody and everybody!

On my journey, I discovered The Leslie Flint Trust (1997-2022). Leslie Flint was a well-recognised medium, well known for his many voice box recordings. These recordings helped me to understand the Spirit World in more detail, which includes the following information. The lower level of the Spirit World is where people go to on their passing. They will be given a chance to consider their lives, and they will experience how their life impacted on other people's lives. They will also be given the chance to stop at this level or whether to progress to higher levels, where they no longer crave Earthly possessions. In spirit, you will have the same characteristics as you did on the Earthly plane.

There are now people in the world who can give guidance on spirit happenings. Nobody needs to be scared to talk about spiritual issues any longer. However, you do still need to be mindful to talk to people who have knowledge of the same, as there are still many doubters in the world – people who are scared, people who want to follow the crowd in their understandings and beliefs. There are still many people who 'fear' hearing voices. They should be embracing their inner voice and not fear the same. Some of the spirits that came through Leslie Flint admitted that they were scared to tell people in their time that they were getting their inspiration from spirit.

There are also many things that can hold you back when you are trying to unfold. Lack of knowledge breeds fear, and that is why it is important not to listen to the wrong people when learning about spiritualism. It is important to surround yourself with love, love from spirit and love from people who understand about spirit.

To improve your knowledge of spiritualism, I would suggest that you visit a local Spiritualist Church as a starting point, read books by recognised people in the field and have readings by the many gifted mediums in the world today, such as those on the Arthur Findlay College website.

They provide two types of readings at the Arthur Findlay College: evidential and assessment. The 'evidential' is a link to your loved ones and the assessment is a 'spiritual assessment' where the medium links to your spirit guides for guidance on your spiritual journey and abilities. It was from one of these assessments that I was able to confirm elements of my journey. I was not just willing to accept my own spirit messages, I wanted confirmation from world-class recognised mediums, as my experience in the legal profession had taught me to get proof to back up situations.

After two unfoldments, I was completely sure of my spiritual journey, which was to understand my own unfoldment so that I could help others with theirs.

I hope that you will not be scared to ask for guidance to help you discover your true spiritual path. Remember, everyone can ask spirit for guidance at any time. You do have to learn to trust your messages though, which is not easy, and that is the reason I used to get readings to back up what spirit were telling me.

3

Childhood

I was born on 7th September 1965, a Virgo, to a normal, average couple who had worked all their lives.

My parents had no educational background themselves, so consequently they could only help with this as far as they were able. They were caring parents, but it was obvious that their judgments were based on their background, and they were steadfast in their beliefs, with no imagination. They were also not religious in any way, and could not understand why I was always talking about God. They had respect for the church as an institution, but they did not need religion in their life like I did.

I remember hearing them talk about me from my bedroom upstairs, saying that they were worried about my obsession with God. I used to listen intently to what they said, but I did not let their opinions get in the way of what I believed in. I was steadfast in my belief, even from a young age, but I did not know why. I just accepted my belief without question.

At school, teachers were quick to notice my lack of confidence, but did not question this, or offer any advice as to how to help me. This subsequently had an impact on my communication skills and my schoolwork. I believe now that even if I had had better communication skills to be able to tell my parents what was going on in my head at that time, they would not have taken me seriously. Their beliefs were tied to their parents' beliefs, and that is how the world turns now. Many people are tied to their past and scared of having their own thoughts and beliefs.

As a child, I had a wild, vivid imagination. I used to hide under the bedclothes, be scared about what was under my bed and imagine there were 'little flying witches' in my garden. You might say that this is normal for a child, but in my case my fear meant that I was experiencing things that only certain people could have understood and helped me with. I realise now that I was letting my own imagination scare me and that this hindered my development. My fear followed me for most of my adult life.

It wasn't until my second unfoldment, many years later, that Sutton Coldfield Spiritualist Church helped me realise I had been listening to spirit all my life and I had been shutting out the noise in my head by constantly listening to music. My mother also should not have let me watch those horror films as a child either, as they certainly did not help – they just scared me even more. I would add here that the problem with horror films is that they infect the true message of spirituality by providing false information.

Living in a fantasy world also impacted on my life. It was in these dreams that I began my journey of communicating with spirit who I now realise filled my head with information I often did not understand. One spirit dream that stands out for me is when I was told the name of my future husband and that he would treat me badly. As I did not realise where these messages were coming from, nor the significance they would have on my life, I did not listen to the same and subsequently I would try to block them out and forget them – only to be reminded of them years later by spirit to make sense of my journey. I now know that the reason spirit wanted me to remember my past was so that I could understand my future, to help other people with theirs!

I must add here that there is a difference between normal dreams and spirit dreams, which is what I had occasionally. When you have a spirit dream, you never forget it. I still remember mine from 12 years ago, but ordinary dreams come and go overnight. I would suggest that you have a notebook and pen at the side of your bed just in case you have a significant dream, as spirit often talk to people in their dreams, even if they are not a medium!

Part of my living in a dreamworld involved shutting myself in my bedroom as I felt that was my 'haven'. Consequently, I became an extremely scared, quiet child, not able to tell the world what I was experiencing. No-one knew what was in my head because I had not learnt how to release the same by communication.

Now, I must address the issue of my incessant dancing as a child, which I now recognise as my attempt to block spirit messages from my mind because I was scared.

My father would hear my tiny feet stomping on the floor above him when he was trying to watch television or read his newspaper. I now know that I was trying to block out the noise in my head of spirit communication, and I consequently became obsessed with dancing, to the detriment of my schoolwork. All the world could see was that I was 'quiet' and that I was a good dancer, which two facts contradicted each other, but were not questioned. If ever you recognise this contradictory behaviour in your child, you should seek guidance, as this was a tell-tale sign for me that I had communication issues which stayed with me most of my life. Spotting unusual behaviour early is important with children.

On the dance floor, I could be who I wanted to be, and no-one questioned how dancing might have had had an impact on my schoolwork. The fact that I was so quiet was also not questioned. What people did notice was that I was an excellent dancer, so I continued with dancing, stomping my little feet wherever I could. The dance floor was the only place that I felt happy at that time of my life, the only place I could retreat into my little world. No-one made the connection between my dancing and my quietness. My obsession with dancing consequently had an impact on my schoolwork, but that didn't worry me, as I lived for dancing and did not think about my future. How could I think about my future when I had so much happening inside my head?

When people saw me for the first time on a dance floor, they thought I had been taking dancing lessons, which of course I hadn't, because my parents would not have been able to afford them. I now know what I was doing was blocking out messages in my head, and I also now believe that I was learning about energies surrounding my body and learning to communicate with my higher self. Remember, I did not know what a medium was at that age, and I did not know about spirit unfortunately, but what I do realise is that I have always had an inner 'knowing' of matters without having experience of the same. I only recognise such things now because, much later in life, spirit made me aware that they had been encouraging me to remember the whole of my life to relay this story to others to help them understand their unfoldment.

Even though I did not understand my experiences as a child, I believed in what I felt, which appeared real to me. However, I could not tell anyone about what I was experiencing, as I was so scared. I believe that if I had of trusted my inner voice at that time it might have stopped me making mistakes in my life which led me down the wrong path. However, it is hard to talk about what you do not understand, so it is important to realise that children need help interpreting their thoughts and beliefs as these can hold them back if they are scared. That's what happened to me. It is important to consider what they say, even if this does not appear to make sense, as they could be sensing spirit like I did. If this is the case, you will need to visit a Spiritualist Church because the medical profession does not accept such things! I did not believe in my inner voices as a child, so consequently I did not follow the advice that I was given, and this subsequently led me down the wrong pathway.

Apart from devoting my time to dancing, I have very bad eyesight which also affected my confidence and held me back. My glasses used to be so thick that they pulled my head down, making me appear more shy than I was. I can remember being too scared to tell my teachers when I couldn't see things in class, but in hindsight, I do not understand why I was scared.

Teachers should have questioned why I was so quiet and recognised that I was crying out for help. The only way that I had learnt to communicate with the world at this time was through dance.

I was also bullied at school. I became aware that rumours were being said around my school about my parents, due to jealousy, and for some reason those rumours were being believed by my classmates. This was also another reason why I was quiet. I was not brave or strong enough to stand up to my bullies, so I just retreated further into my own little world, my fantasy world, where no-one could hurt me!

My final hurdle was that I was not aware as a child that I was developing into a medium, and that the inner voice inside my head was the voice of spirit trying to guide me with my life. If I had believed this, I now know that my life would have taken a different direction. However, in my case, even if my parents had understood or believed what was happening to me, that I was developing into a medium, I believe they would not have known where to get help!

It is important for parents to recognise if their child is not fitting in with the surroundings that they are in, as they might not get the help that they need until many years down the line. There is also a risk that a child may be misdiagnosed as having mental health issues, as doctors seem to be fearful when people say that they are listening to 'voices' in their head. Why are doctors so scared of people listening to their own voice?

It is hard for some people to accept that spirit exists around us, so consequently they may not want to talk about it. I have tried to talk to my sister about messages from our deceased mother, but I can see the non-acceptance on her face.

Another issue with children is that they learn from the actions and words of their parents, so if their parents are blocking themselves from accepting spirit, they might – without intention – offload their disbelief onto their children. Also, if children are brave enough to talk about anything to do with the spirit, their parents might not know where to get help. I would suggest going to your local Spiritualist Church for such matters.

I now recognise that my main issues as a young child were that I feared what was inside my head and this subsequently held me back for many years because I had to understand everything myself before I could help others!

When a child is quiet and unable to communicate, for whatever reason, this can hinder their life. Therefore, it is the duty of parents to try to look out for anything that might be holding their child back. My tell-tale signs were my incessant dancing and quietness, which consequently led to my lack of self-belief. I believe that if someone had encouraged me to talk as a child, then I would not have had so many life problems. My story might have been hard to understand, but it was my life, and what was in my head appeared real to me!

The moral of my story is that we must all listen to each other's stories, no matter how far-fetched they may be, as you never know what the truth is until you hear it, and consider it for what it is! You cannot put spiritual experiences in a box, they are different for everyone, and that is why it is important that they are talked about, to prevent fear. There may be similarities with psychic phenomena, but experiences are individual and subjective, which is why they need to be talked about!

I end my childhood memories by struggling to cope in secondary school due to my communication problems and not recognising that my inner voice was trying to guide me with my life journey. I did not start to understand this until I went to college, where people started to believe in my abilities.

Parents and teachers are in positions of trust so they should make themselves aware of what is normal for the child over which they have control. Remember, every child's experience of life is different, and if they offload to parents or teachers that something has unsettled them, they should seek help on behalf of the child.

4

My college days

I fondly remember my college days as happy ones, and the beginning of when I started to believe in myself and develop into a confident young lady. I don't remember any spiritual messages during that period, but what I do remember is a few strange occurrences which at the time had no rational explanation.

After finishing secondary school, I felt demoralised when I only got a couple of GCSEs. From somewhere, I got the idea that I wanted to be a secretary, so I embarked on a Private Secretarial Course at Sutton Coldfield College. Looking back, as my confidence was low at that time, I was not in the best place to make a life-changing decision. If you recognise that your child has an important decision in life, I suggest that you make sure that they fully understand the consequences of their decision so that they do not regret it years down the line, which is what I did.

With my smartest suit on, I went to an interview to be enrolled on this course, but I was told that I could only be accepted if there was a spare space at the time of the induction. It was clear that the teacher in charge was only taking in Sutton Coldfield's grammar schoolgirls with a string of qualifications to their names, but I was determined not to let this stop me from gaining a place.

The induction day arrived, and I was delighted when I was allowed to join the course. The class was small, with very attentive teachers who obviously loved their job.

I sailed through my first year of the course because I had teachers and friends who believed in me and gave me the confidence to succeed. My newfound self-belief bore fruit and inspired me to fight the good fight with this career. My success proves the value of having good teachers and friends to share experiences with. All students are different, and they all require different environments and methods of teaching. I found out that I performed better in a small class, but all children have different learning requirements. If your child is failing in one environment, you should consider whether that environment should be changed.

I made loads of friends who had better qualifications than myself which considerably rebuilt my confidence. I also won the hearts of my teachers who said that I was an excellent example to the rest of the class. During that time, everything came so easily to me, which was strange considering how I had struggled at school. Due to my increased self-belief in my abilities, I consequently passed every exam, except a couple of the more advanced ones.

One of the main subjects on this course was shorthand, and I remember that this class was always fast and furious. We were being trained to be accurate transcribers of information. We would first be given a passage to learn and then our teacher would read out the passage which we had to write in shorthand. We then had to transcribe the same passage as quickly as possible – timed by her.

One day something odd occurred. As usual, we were called upon to learn a passage and once we had all written it in Pitman Shorthand, the teacher would go around class and ask certain people to read out what they had written. I was chosen on one occasion, but instead of reading out the contents of the passage, strange words came out of my mouth. The teacher tried to get her stopwatch out, but she did not bother to use it, obviously not believing what she had heard! What I consider was strange about this incident is that she never questioned my behaviour on that day, nor did any of my friends (of which were many) ask me what had been going on!

I have been trying to understand what happened that day for years and the only conclusion I have come to is that I was speaking tongues. I have since researched the meaning of this. In The Bible Acts 2:4, speaking in tongues is initial evidence or sign of the baptism of the Holy Spirit.

'And they were filled with the Holy Ghost, and began to speak with other tongues, as the Spirit gave them utterance.'

Exam time came around quickly, and we were all entered for many exams in order that we could achieve as many as possible. My secondary school had not taught me how to prepare for exams, but the college did, and I felt fully prepared and equipped for anything that would come my way. They taught me the importance of working through past papers which is the most important thing that any student should do.

If your child has exams before them, I recommend looking at previous exam papers at the start of their course as this allows them to become familiar with the format which takes away much of the fear and stigma.

During the period of my exams, I experienced another odd occurrence. This happened during a particular three-hour exam. I started the paper and then appeared to put myself in some sort of trance. When I came out of the trance, I found that the three allotted hours were over. This happened a few times at college. Although I can remember these occurrences clearly, I did not understand their significance at the time, but I never forgot what happened, as it was so strange!

I sailed through my first year at college and gained a vast array of qualifications. They trained us hard, and I responded well to the good teaching and small classes.

During the second year of college, I met my ex-husband, so my attention was slightly steered towards him rather than studying. This didn't matter so much as I had worked so hard in my first year that my lapse of attention on this second year did not really matter. My teachers were concerned at my slight dip in grades, but this concern was proved to be unfounded as I had worked hard enough in my first year to carry me through. I appeared to no longer have the communication issues that I had as a child. My teachers believed in me, and my parents were proud that I had succeeded in preparing myself for a worthwhile career.

At the end of this course, the lady who had interviewed me two years before who did not want to take me on the course, now relayed her apologies as I was the only student in the class that had passed everything, which was incredible considering my fellow students were all more qualified than I was.

With a trail of qualifications in my back pocket and my new-found confident personality, I went out into the big wide world with renewed vigour!

5

My working life

My collection of qualifications and my new-found confidence gained me a good career within the legal profession, which lasted over 20 years. However, despite my success I could never understand why I was never satisfied and continually felt the need to jump from job to job. This habit started to make my cv harder and harder to explain, because I did not understand my behaviour myself. I also did not understand why, even after a full day at work, I would still want to race home, searching for new life directions – not just career-wise, but in relationships, too.

As time passed, I recognised that when I was respected by a firm I was working for, people noticed I was capable of so much more and would question why I was still a secretary. But when I was working for firms that did not respect me, I became totally bored and struggled to even do the most mundane secretarial work. Another reason that I was at times unhappy was that I would often find myself victim to ruthless people, due to my sensitive nature and would end up leaving firms even when I enjoyed the job. I had a big heart, and I was used and abused in the city by a lot of ruthless people.

Despite whether I felt happy or unhappy where I worked, it was clear that I was always loved and respected by the people that I worked with, which I did not discover until years later. I believe this was because over the years I had learnt how to treat people and even though I was ambitious I would never tread on anyone's toes. Years later, one of my work colleagues came back through a medium to tell me how much she respected me. This touched me, as I never had time for friends due to the busy environment I worked in, but this lady remembered me and came back to relay her love and respect years later.

When I reflect on the various managers that I worked for throughout my career, I noticed that I seemed to have better relations with managers when I was working close to them – something I could not understand. I now know that I was using my psychic ability to climatise myself, not only with my manager but also with the whole firm. Some of my managers often wondered how I knew things, which I could not explain. I had wild ideas in my head that I must be psychic, but it was many years after that I discovered that I was. I now appreciate the importance of managers who believe in your abilities and how important it is to protect one's vulnerability.

My last manager believed in me, but he could not fight my corner because I had written him an email using my spirit writing, which concerned him. No-one understood my spirit writing at that time, so no-one could help me. I know that it hurt him to let me go as he recognised the connection that we had. However, only I knew that our connection was a spiritual one which would have been hard for him to understand as solicitors are not allowed to believe in spiritual matters.

I lost two jobs due to my spirit writing. Despite my last two employers trying to help me, they did not know how to, as I had too much going on in my mind and could not control what I was saying or writing, which meant I was misunderstood. Despite losing my career in the legal profession, I had gained some valuable skills which would stay with me for the rest of my life. The skills that I had gained using my hands over the years were later used by spirit to communicate with the world!

6

Motherhood

I was working at Anthony Collins Solicitors in Birmingham when I discovered I was pregnant with my son. I collapsed on a bus on the way to work, and after medical examinations I was told that I was six months pregnant. This was a tremendous shock to the whole of my family because they all knew how much I valued my career and that I was not planning to have children. What they did not know was that I had an inner yearning for a child, without even realising it. This is an example of why you should always listen to what your body is telling you, as it has a voice of its own!

The morning after I collapsed, I noticed that my belly seemed to have grown overnight. I instantly accepted what was ahead, as I knew that this was meant to be. The first thought in my head was: who was I not to give this child a chance in life?

During the same period, I experienced a strange occurrence at this firm. After notifying Human Resources of my pregnancy, the senior partner approached me and put his hands on my tummy and said, 'God bless you.'

I thought this very odd at the time, but I have pondered on this and all I can come up with is that he saw my light, just like my grandmother did. Why else would a senior partner of a large firm in the city do such a thing? I now realise that for him to make a spiritual connection with me means that he must have been a very special man himself.

The lead-up to taking maternity leave was a happy time in my life. I was excited to meet up with my work colleagues and enjoyed listening to other mother's experiences. I finally had a common interest to share! I confessed how scared I was about having a child and one friend reassured me that there would be lots of people around me at the hospital helping me at the birth. This comment gave me all the reassurance that I needed!

I had my son one month early. As I only discovered that I was pregnant at six months, I was only aware of his existence for 2 months! I had a difficult birth, which was mainly fuelled by my fear of labour – something I know many women will relate to. After a long labour, the midwife suggested that forceps be used, but I would not allow this, as I had heard too many bad stories about forceps damaging the baby's head. Instead, I begged them to do a C-section, which they did.

I was high on gas and air at the time and would not let go of the receptacle because I was so scared. I was subsequently moved to the operating theatre to have my C-section, and whilst on the operating table, I could feel blood leaving my body. I remember spirit approaching me and I said deep within my mind that I would die for my son and spirit replied that it was not my time! I now believe that this was a near-death experience for me.

On 11th November 1997, my son Alex was born. He was tiny, but perfect in every way. From the moment I held him in one hand, I could feel the potential of this little man. He was my own 'little star', who put me in favour again with my ex-husband for a short time. I now recognise that I had feared giving birth to a child and that was the reason for my denial of wanting a child until then.

My maternity leave came and went. These days, women get a year, but at the time I had my son I was only allowed two months off. I had to finish work a month before my maternity leave was due because I was suffering with backache, so in the end I only had one month's maternity leave.

Like all new mothers, I enjoyed my maternity leave, pottering around my house, doing jobs that I never normally had time to do because I was always working, and often too tired to do anything when I got home. I would have loved to continue being a 'stay at home' mom but my ex-husband encouraged me to return, so back to work I went with a heavy heart!

Time passed quickly and before long my son was a toddler. I found it frustrating when he couldn't talk to me, but I knew I had to be patient as every parent needs to be with a young child. Parents should remember that just because children cannot talk does not mean they are not receptive of what is being said to them. When he did start to talk, it was amazing. I was truly a proud mother and I paid close attention to anything he was having problems with so that he would not encounter the same hurdles in his life that I had.

I noticed that from a young age he had problems holding a pen, but I did not know at the time how to help him with this. I also recognised that he was a quiet child, as I had been. I realised that I needed to address this because I was only too aware how communication issues had impacted on my life, and I did not want the same for him. To address this, I found a local football team for youngsters, where he immediately fitted in – all his friends loved him – and he proved to be quite the little star on the football pitch. His grandfather would occasionally, when he was well, go along to watch and cheer him on. After joining the team, my son's communication skills developed in spades, and it was clear he had a mind of his own from a young age!

My son had changed my life forever. I was now a mellower person, and it was clear that my life would never return to how it had been, and I didn't want it to!

7

Mistakes people made about me

Before losing two positions in the legal profession, I was sent on numerous occasions to sit before various doctors to diagnose me. The first time was before a team of doctors, with my dear departed father alongside me. My father tried to tell them that he believed it was the conditions in which I lived which had impacted on my mental health, but they would not listen to him. They ordered him out of the room and continued to scare me with their pre-conditioned questions. Unfortunately, as I was so afraid, I could not speak clearly so I was misdiagnosed with a mental health condition.

Years later, a nurse who had been in the group at the time, visited my house and told me that there had been arguments amongst them when they were trying to diagnose me. Some of the team had apparently questioned why I was repeatedly saying the same things again and again, which they believed meant something. However, the head doctor wouldn't listen to his team and his misdiagnosis of my having a mental health condition stayed with me – not only in a thick file but plastered across my life thereafter. I knew that meant

I would never work again in the 'material' world. I also knew there was no point questioning this, so I just accepted it, and put it to the back of my mind. I might have lost my career, but no-one could stop me believing that spirit was now working with me!

The many things which my doctors should have considered about me included my troubled childhood, losing my career in the legal profession and the imminent breakdown of my marriage. I also had spirit encounters, but I knew they would not have listened to this! I now realise that even if I had been able to communicate to the world when I was young or when I was before a team of doctors that misdiagnosed me, it is doubtful whether they would have listened to what I had to say. They had a list of pre-conditioned questions before them, based on the diagnosis of previous patients, and it was obvious that they would not consider anything else outside the box.

I believe that these kinds of misdiagnoses frequently happen due to the medical profession's inability to understand 'spiritual' matters and the connection to the physical existence. The spirit existence can live without the physical ('death'), but the physical existence cannot exist without the spirit!

What was not normal to the real world was normal to me! Spiritual work was now part of my life, and I did not really care whether people believed me or not. I now believed in my mediumistic abilities, and I was determined to continue with my new-found spiritual path.

No-one should be scared to stand up for what they believe in. Your beliefs are yours! Do not let anyone tell you different!

8

My experience of being homeless

I had never experienced homelessness before; this was my first time. I had lost my job and my family due to my spirit writing. I knew that I could no longer stay in the matrimonial home as there were too many bad vibes floating around between my ex-husband and myself. We had widespread plumbing issues around our house at that time, which made me wonder if they were the result of poltergeist activity, but I never proved this. I have provided a chapter on ghost activity, which includes poltergeist activity, to help readers consider the same. Years later, I asked the advice of Jean Kelford (medium) about these experiences, and she also said that it sounded like poltergeist activity.

Due to my desperation, the local council managed to secure temporary accommodation at a hotel in Edgbaston for me, who had dedicated a wing to homeless people. When I learned of my placement, I threw my clothes and limited possessions into two suitcases and jumped into the back of a taxi. I told the taxi driver to keep my location private as I was scared my ex-husband would follow me to my new location. He had done that before when he was trying to discover where I had been going to when I visited Sutton Spiritualist Church at the time of my first unfoldment.

I did not tell anyone where I had run away to, not even my parents. I needed time to sort myself out and I knew my parents would understand this.

I arrived like a gypsy, dishevelled, and shaking. After filling in a long form for benefit purposes, I was directed to my new home – one tiny room. Although I was frightened, I felt safe there, as I was finally free of my ex-husband's control. I set up my computer on my desk in the room and carried on with my journey of self-discovery without interference from the outside world.

I continued to sort out my Earthly problems one by one and kept working on my confidence building and self-discovery. Although I was hoping to make some friends at my new 'home', the people that were there were too troubled and had their own issues to sort out. They appeared not want to make friends, so I decided to keep myself to myself.

One night, a very troubled lady, with mental health issues, knocked on my door and begged me to give her money to return to her partner. I quickly concluded that I should not help her as he had been violent towards her. I also had to pull the telephone line out of the wall as I was receiving scary telephone calls from fellow residents. Although it was quite frightening living in an environment full of people with mental health, drink, and drug issues, it was not as scary as the vibes that had been floating around my matrimonial home.

Time passed quickly whilst I was there. I plodded along day by day, filling my time sorting out my Earthly problems. I knew spirit were with me, as I would frequently get images of numbers on hotel doors in my mind when spirit was warning me that the hotel would be moving me into other rooms. I was now aware that the visions that I had experienced always came true and I would never doubt them again!

Some examples of visions that I had included seeing a male friend on the bow of a ship, feeling very happy and content, as he looked out to sea. He confirmed what I said, but he had problems taking the ship. I explained to him that the ship represented his life journey. Another vision from my past, which I had predicted years before, was where I saw myself in the hotel room where I was now living.

After being in my small hotel room for approximately three months, a lady banged on my door and pushed herself into my tiny room. She told me I had to get out and she threw my meagre possessions into my suitcases and told me to leave. What people do not realise is that when a homeless person is provided with temporary accommodation at these safe houses, it is only 'temporary', and they can be thrown out after a short time.

I remember seeing one lady returning to being homeless with her meagre possessions in black bags and thinking how sad it was. Fortunately, I did have a lifeline, as I knew that my parents would help me if I was desperate, and I was! They did not have a spare bedroom, so I had to sleep on their living room floor, but it was better than being on the streets where many people end up after they have suffered tragedy in their lives.

It was not long before I was notified that the council had found a local flat for me, so thankfully that ended my homeless experience. If anyone is ever in such a desperate situation, I would suggest that they seek guidance from housing charities or their local council.

I was fortunate to be able to draw a line in the sand as to my homeless situation, but there are many people who never find such help and end up on the streets where it becomes difficult to escape from. Whenever I see people sleeping in doorways and cardboard boxes, I remember my time of being homelessness and thank God that my situation was only temporary!

9

My first unfoldment

At the time of my first unfoldment, my ancestors (which included my grandmother) visited me in a spirit dream as they wanted me to understand what had occurred in the past, so that history did not repeat itself any longer. In that dream, I was told that they believed they had 'influence' over people, and that they felt guilty that people would give them things because they loved them. They told me that the family was allowed to earn a living, but they must not take advantage of the influence that they believed they had.

My grandmother also told me that when I was a child, I might have thought that she did not love me. She made it clear to me that this was not the case and explained that the reason she found it hard to look at me was because my light was so bright. She told me that people would be drawn to me like a moth to a candle when they were crying out for help, and that it was a family trait. I knew this was true because people had frequently told me about my light throughout my journey! It took me a while before I understood what my grandmother meant by 'influence', but I did recognise that people were being drawn to me!

After this dream, my first unfoldment began. I started experiencing strange occurrences, like my spirit writing all night, seeing light coming from my hands in a mirror in a dark room and seeing my grandmother's face transfigure over mine. My grandmother had also warned me that I would be seeing spirit soon, and not to be scared. She also directed me to Sutton Spiritualist Church for guidance.

It was at this church where I experienced a table tilting incident, where a table rose into the air and my grandmother spoke to me clearly for the first time. It was the first time that I became aware of spirit energy around me, and from that moment I knew that everything that had been foretold to me in my spirit dream was true, and that my life was changing beyond all recognition. I was so happy that my dreams had turned into reality, but I was sad because I knew that my life would never be the same again. I felt like a chrysalis before it opens out into a butterfly. I knew the future would be amazing, but I did not know what was going to come out, just like a butterfly does not know what is going to happen to it – it just accepts!

I had accepted spirit into my life and there was no way of going back. This was now who I was. I realised that there was a risk that the world might not understand what I was telling them, but I knew that it was part of my journey to use my abilities to help others with theirs, so I had to forget about any fear that I had and move forwards into the bright sunlight, sharing my knowledge with anyone and everyone who would listen to me!

Using my 'inner knowing' mediumship, I understood that years ago people were not so knowledgeable about spiritual matters, and what my ancestors had feared was not 'influence' but 'mediumship'. They had been open to spirit all the time, which is why they were perceived as being 'good people'. Their spiritual light had shone onto the world, like mine did, drawing people in need to them, just like my grandmother told me that I would. I now believe that it was this light which had been recognised by the senior partner when I was pregnant!

My ancestors' lack of knowledge, however, had caused misunderstandings and misconceptions going back generations. So, in essence, not knowing about a 'gift' can be worse than 'knowing' because if you know at least you can learn how to use that gift.

In trying to unravel the truth, I discovered that some members of the family had not been told of their abilities, which had caused them problems throughout their lives. I came to this conclusion after being told by one of my uncles (whilst he was alive) that my mother was one of the family members who was not told, and she had experienced problems throughout her life because she was not able to use her gift to protect herself. I am sure that my grandmother would not have deliberately caused her children to have the wrong information. I believe that in her day people did not understand enough about mediumship, so this had caused issues going back generations. This is a clear example of how lack of information can cause problems.

Even from a young age, I had felt a presence from my mother's side of the family. I now understood that it was this presence that made them fearful they were influencing people, when in fact they were just open to spirit, which was attracting people to them. My ancestors feared this presence, just like I did when

I first felt it. It was now clear to me that I had inherited this family presence, and it was this that had been felt by my work colleagues in the city which made them all love me.

When my last manager had been trying to help me, he told me I had made more of an impact in one year than he had done in five years! This amazed him and was one of the reasons why he tried to fight for my retention in that firm. Unfortunately, I was unable to tell the world clearly what was happening to me as I feared telling the truth. As a result, no-one was able to help me.

I never believed for a second that the family's presence was bad, and that made me even more determined to discover the truth. Fear can be a terrible thing. I wanted the fear to end, and to restore not just mine, but my family's name. What I clung onto was the fact that I knew my ancestors had been good people, along with the fact that 'no-one can influence anyone'! They were simply good people, who were attracting people to them for guidance, just like my grandmother said to me about moths being drawn to a flame. This message from my grandmother of 'moths to flame' also made me conclude that I was not dealing with a bad situation.

The final message my ancestors told me was that I was now that 'flame'. I was told that I was the only one who could put matters right with my spiritual knowledge to help people understand spiritual matters and not to fear their unfoldment (development).

If my ancestors had not made me aware of my mediumistic abilities via my spirit dream 12 years ago, and had I not learnt how to use my ability, I would not have discovered my spiritual pathway to help others with their spiritual unfoldment. I would also not have unearthed the family mystery which had caused misunderstandings and disharmony within my mother's family going back generations. One Arthur Findlay medium had told me that I was now flying the flag for my family, who gathered around me to make clear misunderstandings. People were scared in the past of experiencing spiritual phenomena, but now that time has passed, and they should no longer be scared!

10

Discovering ECSC

After another long search for answers, I was pleased to find Erdington Christian Spiritualist Church. From the moment I walked into this little church, Linda Wilson walked over to me and hugged me, I felt truly loved. The love that I felt was not just from the members of this church, but also from spirit. This love was pure. It was breath-taking. Consequently, I started to go to this church regularly and I made many lovely friends. What I admired the most was that nobody complained if the mediums had a bad night there. All that was important was that the church was filled with the love of 'God'.

I started my spiritual journey reading spiritual texts at their Sunday services, and I quickly became aware that I was connecting to spirit when I was reading. Reading made me very happy, and I sang out the Lord's praises with everything I read.

At one service, Eddie Cullen (now deceased), who was an experienced medium, was inspired when I read a passage and he said out aloud that the Lord would be using my voice soon. Years later, I now know that he was right, and here I am writing this book, using my voice to help people realise that spirit guidance is there if you need it! Remember, we all have free will, so it is up to us whether we accept any spirit guidance that we receive.

After visiting Erdington Christian Spiritualist Church for a while, I discovered their Pilgrim's Progress Workshop Spiritualist Course, which was a spiritual enlightenment course. I would suggest that if you are considering whether a spiritual course is suitable that you understand what it entails, and perhaps talk to members of the church who have done the course to see whether it is suitable for you. I later became aware that it is not always clear what spiritual courses entail.

From the moment I was asked to stand on the rostrum, I could not believe how good I felt, sharing my life experiences with the congregation. I finally felt that I was putting my life experiences to good use. I also felt that this was a healing experience for me. I was elated that people listened to me and valued what I said. I now believe that spirit had led me into the city to build up my skillset so that I could help others. Spirit knew what a good communicator I was, and wanted me to put my gifts to good use. Spirit will help you with your life journey, if you ask them, but you do need to work for your dreams!

I progressed well on their Pilgrims Progress Course, and I soon became aware that my 'hands' were 'my thing'. Consequently, I became proficient in ribbon reading, which was witnessed by the congregation at Erdington Christian Spiritualist Church on various occasions. As soon as I picked the ribbons up, I could feel the energy flowing through my fingers. The best reading that I did was for a man, who had been a medium the whole of his life, and he told me that he had never experienced anyone using ribbons the way I did! I was a bit scared when I gave this reading because I blacked out when I gave this message. I was an inexperienced medium at this time, and this experience surprised and shocked me. After talking to experienced mediums since, it appears that this is a normal experience. This experience did, however, provide me with further evidence of how spirit was working with me. Unfortunately, however, when the church asked me to drop the ribbons to give links, I could not do it as I had become 'deeply' attached to the ribbons.

What I did not understand at this time, was that I was struggling to make links to spirit on the rostrum without my ribbons. I was aware that I was seeing spirit, but I did not realise the importance of 'talking' to spirit. I now understand that it is important to remember that spirits are people who want to communicate, so it is important to talk to them.

Although I had enjoyed my time at Erdington Church and gained very valuable skills, I felt a yearning to progress with my knowledge. I strongly believe that spirit at this time inspired me to do a degree to help me understand and improve my communication skills. I was once again doing things 'for a purpose' - something one manager had made me aware of in the past.

Unfortunately, when I tried to return to Erdington Church, after I finished my degree 5 years later, it was at the time of Covid-19, and they were struggling to keep their doors open. My little church, in my absence, had been going downhill.

My only option now was to return to Sutton Coldfield Spiritualist Church after a long period away. If I had not trusted my feelings to return there, I would have lost the chance to meet some lovely people and begin my journey properly, with love in my heart!

11

Sensing grief for the first time

I did not understand the pain of death until I lost my parents. First, my father, then my mother. One by one, my relatives were passing away. As each one passed, I became aware that my messages first came from my grandmother, then my father, and then my mother, in that order - not just to me but also through other mediums. Even though I now believed in my messages, I had developed a habit of constantly checking my messages against other medium's messages, a habit which I still have not broken away from!

There were many times in my life when I had not got on well with my mother, but since her passing, I now believe that I can hear her clearer than ever. She was finally talking and not shouting at me, and because of this I was now listening to every word she said to me. When I was a child, she would shout and strut her stuff in front of me like a peacock, but now she came through with 'love' and I 'listened'. Of course, I always knew that she did love me, but her shouting made me recoil into my shell, and I developed a flight response whenever she shouted at me, which is the same as animals do when they feel that they are in danger.

From listening to my experiences, I am sure that any parents amongst you can recognise that it is important for them to be careful, not only with what they say to their children, but also in the way they say it, as harsh words can impact on your child's confidence, which can affect their whole life. It is important to try and stop mistakes and misunderstandings before they happen, as they might be harder to rectify years later.

From the many messages that came through for me from my parents, it was obvious that they realised that they had made mistakes with me, and it was clear that they were trying their utmost to put things right.

Whilst attending a séance for the first time (performed by a well-known medium) my mother spoke about how she was proud of me, and how much she loved me, but she did wish she could have supported me through 'difficult times'. In reply, I told her that she did help me in the end, and that is what mattered. I was so happy to hear my mother's voice again - not the overbearing mother that used to shout to me that I did not listen to, but a more compassionate mother. As a result of this message, and many others which came through various mediums, I received a constant stream of love and guidance which subsequently helped me with my grief and my understanding of my journey.

Do not be worried about causing spirits harm when they come to give you messages. They are just as relieved to talk to you again as you are to talk to them. Allowing them to come through to say sorry gives them relief which will allow them to progress in the Spirit World, should they wish to.

My belief in the afterlife grew even more after receiving all the lovely messages from my parents and my grandparents. I always believed that my mother would be the one in charge, and I was right. My grandmother rarely came through after the death of my parents, which proved to me that the reins had been handed over to my mother. Now that I believe in my spirit messages, I am now able to communicate freely with my family whenever I wish - mainly my mother. It is like they are still 'alive', only better. My mother now spoke to me from the heart in a way that she never did in her lifetime, and this has made me love her in a different way, more than I ever did before!

If you want to hear your relatives in the Spirit World, I advise you visit a local Spiritualist Church and when you attend make sure that you 'listen' to messages that come through. I would suggest that if you wish to receive messages from your relatives that you give them permission to come through, as they do need your permission! It is also useful to note these messages down (if this is not done by a scribe during services) so that you can make sense of them later. Another way of communicating with your relatives is by listening to your dreams, as spirit will frequently try to use your dreams to communicate, which was how spirit liked to communicate with myself. I would suggest that you think of a question before you go to bed, and wait to see if you get a reply from your ancestors. If they want you to remember the message, you will!

I am now aware that there is no need to grieve as our loved ones are around us, and that everyone – even if you are not a medium – is able to communicate with their loved ones!

12

My second unfoldment

The reason I did not complete my development at my first unfoldment was because I became too scared to proceed, and I did not know who to approach for help. I was also coping with my marriage break-up at the time, so I decided to shut spirit communication down. The fear that I felt during this period was the exact same fear that I used to feel when I was working in the city alongside people I did not feel at ease with. Despite shutting down to spirit for some time, I was aware that they were still trying to assist me by sending various people my way to help me believe in myself and my abilities again.

One lesson that I learnt from my first unfoldment was that it is one thing being aware of an ability and another thing knowing how to use it. It is for this reason that I believe I was directed to return to Sutton Coldfield Spiritualist Church so that I could proceed with my training.

My second unfoldment was sparked when I had the time to devote to my spiritual development, after the death of my parents, as I was no longer tied by Earthly shackles. I now not only believed in my abilities, but

I had the means to continue, due to the hard work of my parents during their lifetime.

On my return to Sutton Coldfield Spiritualist Church, it was clear to me that the atmosphere had changed. It now seemed more welcoming and inviting. I was of course now more receptive to spiritual life with a more positive outlook, so this could be the reason why I felt the atmosphere more inviting.

After six weeks of visiting Sutton Coldfield Spiritualist Church, to my surprise, I received messages from my parents via various mediums every week. No-one knew my story there, so I believe that my messages were genuine. This surprised me as, when I had attended 12 years previously, I never used to get any messages.

These messages mainly consisted of my parents apologising and giving me encouragement that they would back me with whatever I wanted to do with my life. My grandparents also came through with similar messages. These messages were just what I needed to give me the confidence knowing that I had my ancestors' blessings to be a medium. This approval had been playing on my mind since my spirit dream 12 years before when I was warned to only use my ability for good!

During my time with this church, I discovered some amazing workshops and regularly attended anything that was available to improve my spiritual knowledge. However, what I needed most was to develop further as a medium and to learn how to use my mediumistic skill to the best of my ability. Consequently, I decided to join mediumship training with Jean Kelford and Chris Beech, who are both international mediums. I soon learnt that this class was all about linking to spirit in preparation to work on the rostrum. I knew that I had to try to forget what I had learnt in the past and learn how to link the SNU way.

In between my mediumistic training, I continued to go to their Sunday services at this church. One service that I will never forget was when Jacqui Rogers (a well-known medium who could see auras) was the visiting medium. As usual, I sat on the front row, hoping for a message, just the same as everyone else. She immediately homed in on me, telling me how strong my light was. In her words: 'Your light is filling this church. You are amazing!' She then asked, 'Are you a soldier for God?' and I had to admit that I was. If I had said 'No', I would have been turning God away, and I did not want to do this. Her words filled me with love and encouragement. I was overjoyed that someone had finally recognised me for who I was. Someone had seen and recognised my light, just like my grandmother had told me at my first unfoldment. In her words, she had given me the key to my door, which she said was the most that any medium could do. She said that you can give people the key to their door, but you could not make them go through the door.

I continued with my mediumistic training, which went from strength to strength, and as the weeks passed, I gained more and more friends at this church. I enjoyed sharing stories with people who had obviously had similar experiences to myself. As my spiritual knowledge grew, I gained a deeper understanding of the meaning of spiritual philosophy, which is the basis of the religion of spiritualism. Subsequently, I became aware that spirit was directing me to do a healing course at the church to mend fences from the past, and to enable me to move forwards.

13

Need to heal

When I realised that I had hit a barrier with my development and wondered what was holding me back, I concluded that I needed to heal. I knew that I had to get rid of the fear of my development and hurt which I had been holding onto from my past. I realised that it was important to get rid of Earthly baggage to make way for my spiritual awakening.

To bring healing into your life and to invite a spiritual awakening, it is important to focus on your end goal of being healed and what might be getting in the way of that healing. I would suggest that it helps to write these down in a journal and to start to work towards that end goal.

The first thing that you need to do, to invite a spiritual awakening to transform your life, is to declutter to get rid of barriers. It is necessary for you to declutter both your physical and spiritual self to make room for the new you. You need to clear your space of the stuff that you no longer need which serves as a distraction from your life. Decluttering your physical space is a start. Then it is important to declutter your mind. To do this, take time every day to sit in silence and solitude.

Allow your thoughts to pass without judgment and slowly watch your mind clear of mental clutter. Meditation allows you to relax and offers you a greater connection to your intuition which is your spiritual guidance.

Once you have decluttered, it is important to examine your beliefs and be conscious of what you believe. It is important to understand the energy that you are putting out, not only into your world, but into the world at large. It is important to be honest when you consider whether your beliefs are supporting your spiritual growth. Sometimes a spiritual awakening requires letting go of beliefs we have held for most of our entire lives. When considering moving forward to a spiritual awakening, you must first realise that you have been sleeping.

After examining your beliefs, it is important to expand your mind, expand new ideas and differing beliefs. For this, you should read books and attend lectures and have conversations with people who have lived different lives for guidance. An awakening occurs when you have learned something new, when you have 'quite literally' woken your mind, and your spirit awakens from a slumber you perhaps didn't even know you were in. When you expand your mind to allow in new ideas, beliefs, and possibilities, you increase the opportunity to wake up to a life experience you never knew was possible.

After expanding your mind, the next stage is to go outside. There is energy and spirit and magic in the outdoors. So many of us spend our time cooped up inside, sitting behind computer screens, not truly connected to the world (or to ourselves). It is important to take time to connect with nature. Even in the big cities you can find trees to touch, gardens to admire, fresh air to breathe. Try not to distract yourself with your phone, or even another person's company. Give yourself the quiet and the solitude and the presence that comes with being outside. You may be surprised by what comes alive within you!

On your healing journey it is important to take care of yourself by eating healthily and staying active, which are great ways to stay connected to yourself and your 'higher power'.

As soon as you have dealt with issues inside and outside your body, you will be in a better position to move forward with your spiritual awakening and your spiritual journey. Do not be afraid to ask for guidance on your spiritual journey from your local Spiritualist Church, and your Spirit Guides who are always there with you, even if you are not aware that they are!

Understanding the difference between Spiritualist and Magnetic Healing

The essence of spiritualism is to accept the love of spirit for what it is PURE LOVE, and it is this love from God that a healing medium allows to flow through them when they act as a vessel for God's healing energies.

The Spiritualists' National Union (n.d): If someone is training to be a healing medium, it is important to understand the difference between Spiritualist Healing and Magnetic Healing. It is also important for a patient to understand the difference as well, so that they get the healing which they need.

Magnetic Healing

This is the application of energies from a physical source, and not from spirit. It is often mistaken for spiritualist healing. Around every human being, as well as animals, flowers, and all living things, there is a field of force. This is an energy field; its composition is generally thought to be electromagnetic in its structure. It is in this energy field that some clairvoyant mediums see colours in people's aura, auric field, or electromagnetic field. Magnetic healing is merely the transference of this vital bodily energy from a person who has it in abundance to another person who is in a depleted condition. When a healing medium connects with a patient it is natural for them to have an inner sympathy and desire to help. This results in a conscious giving of self to the patient, thus establishing a link or state of rapport. A spiritualist healing medium attunes to the spiritual energies from the God Force, who administers the healing forces that are required. The initial link has served its purpose and is no longer necessary. The reason why some healing mediums feel tired and depleted after a healing session is because they have not attuned to the spirit healing energy, they have tried to direct the healing to where they think it is needed with their own energies, and this depletes them. This means that they have been doing magnetic healing and not spiritualist healing because with spiritualist healing, they would feel energised. Whilst magnetic healing appears to work, in fact, it only lasts a short time, usually for as long as the patient can retain the energies given. Healing mediums should not become emotionally involved with their patients or try to heal patients with their own energy, otherwise their own vital resources will flow out to every patient contacted. This will drain them of their own vitality. Even if the healing mediums are not conscious of any spirit power flowing through, they must remain passive, relaxed, and withdrawn, perfectly confident that spirit is working and in control of where it is needed and aware of what is going on.

Spiritualist Healing

It is most important for a healing medium to learn to understand that they are an intermediary (channel) between spirit and the patient. In trying to understand this connection, it is important for them to learn how to cultivate attunement which consists of a blending with spirit. Attunement is about mentally withdrawing from material conditions, so the conscious part of your brain is less active, allowing the blending to take place. The subconscious brain needs to be switched to a higher spiritual level, and attunement allows this to happen. Spiritual healing energies are at a higher frequency than our own, so it is important to be able to start, maintain and stop this frequency during healing sessions when moving from one patient to another. It is important to understand that the healing medium should not focus on a patient's conditions as this would interfere with attunement. If a healing medium focuses on helping their patient this could mean that magnetic healing is taking place not spiritualist healing. During the attunement, a healing medium must be mentally relaxed and confident. It is also important to end the link before going to a new patient, and you can do this by the washing hands to break the link. It is also important to maintain your link with spirit when you change from one patient to another, but this is an accomplished technique.

It is important for a healing medium to understand the difference between ''spiritualist and 'magnetic healing' so that they allow the healing from the God Force that a patient needs without becoming involved in any way. The healing medium does not need to know whether the correct healing is being given, they just need to accept that they are a channel for the God Force Energies. It is also important for a patient to know the difference as well so that they get the healing energies that they require.

It is important for a healing medium to understand the passive level of consciousness, which is required for healing to be effective, allowing higher levels of the Spirit World to work through them to the patient with whom you are working with. Attunement is important in the act of healing as it shows respect to Spirit by setting intention before and after a healing session, and respect to patients when moving from one patient to another. It is also important to know when Spirit withdraws. Attunement is however personal from one healing medium to another, some might say a prayer, listen to music, etc. Whatever makes them relaxed, and conscious is acceptable. Healing is a very special connection between God, the healing medium, and the patient. The healing energies come from Spirit (God), through the Spirit Healing Guides of the healing medium (who refine the energy) to the patient (who is also spirit). It is there for all who request it – whether you believe in God or not!

14

Predictions

I will now talk about what made me come to the realisation that I was a psychic medium, and that I was connecting to spirit for answers.

As my life unfolded, I recognised that I had experienced many visions and received many messages which later became reality. So, the moral of this story is to listen to your inner voice just in case spirit are trying to direct you with your life journey, which is what happened to me. I believe that spirit was making me remember my life journey to help me understand my unfoldment so that I could help others with theirs!

As a child, I was told in a dream the name of the man that I would marry and that he would treat me badly. Because I was so young when I had this dream, I never paid attention to it. This prediction came true.

Whilst working at various solicitors' offices in the city, I regularly experienced gut instincts when I believed they had problems. As time passed, and I moved from job to job, all my predictions came true one by one.

In a dream, years before the event, I saw myself in a hotel room where my parents visited me. This prediction came true at the time of my marriage breakdown.

In a spirit dream, I saw myself in a journalist's office, trying to get them interested in a story that I had to tell. I did not understand this vision at the time. I told them that I wanted to be published in their newspaper. Of course, they did not listen to what I said. They only wanted an advert from me to advertise my psychic services, after I had told them that I was a psychic medium. Although the meaning of this dream did not make sense to me at the time, it later occurred to me that I was being prepared to give them a story in the future.

Whilst at the last firm that I worked for, I sent in various sick notes. On one sick note that I sent in, for some reason I scribbled that I was going to write a famous book just like J. K. Rowling did with the Harry Potter books. I now believe that I was making the prediction that I was going to write my first book, which is what you are reading now!

At the time of my first unfoldment, my manager said that I did everything for a 'purpose'. I believe that it appeared that I was doing everything for a purpose because I was predicting what was going to happen in the future.

In conclusion, I now believe that all my life spirit had been preparing me with the necessary life skills so that I could share my knowledge of unfoldment with the world!

15

Strange occurences

As my strange occurrences grew throughout my journey, I started to document them. The reason I did this was because at times even I wondered whether I was imagining it all!

I have put these occurrences in approximate date order, so that you can see how they progressed throughout my life and increased with intensity at the time of my first and second unfoldment when I finally concluded that I was a psychic medium. Every experience that I had gave me the confidence to move forward and to believe in myself, and to recognise that my abilities were not all in my head!

Whilst on a holiday with family to Cornwall at a young age, I went out to sea with my father in a small dinghy, the sea was like a mill pond, no sign of waves. A huge wave came from nowhere, and I remember that I blanked out when I plunged into the water. The next thing that I remember is being dragged out of the sea. Then I remember feeling my body coming out of the sea and being aware of the pressure of the water around my body. This was my father who had been frantically diving trying to find me amongst the waves. When he found me, he lifted me up with his strong arms, lifting me up into the air. My father (in spirit) years later came back to give me a message about this incident which was that he would always be with me to hold me up. I believe this was a near-death experience which I never forgot. What interests me is how I blacked out at the time I entered the water. I believe this is what happens when we are approaching death and spirit comes to grab us to take us to the Spirit World. I have read many accounts of people around the world who report similar near-death experiences.

During a shorthand incident at college, when I read out a passage to the class in a strange tongue, no-one said anything to me, and the class continued as if nothing had happened. No one questioned my behaviour either. I still don't understand the significance of this. It was obviously the start of my spiritual life, as this was the first of many spiritual experiences that I had!

Whilst taking three-hour exams at college, and whilst I was studying for my degree, I became aware that during exams I would go blank, and when I came around the exam was over. During one law exam, I finished an hour early and still got a top mark – all without any memory of what I had written! I believe that these strange occurrences were my doing and that somehow, I had learned how to go into a trance. I do not believe these occurrences were spirit-led as I don't believe they would have been allowed to do this. I believe that I had somehow learned how to put myself in a trance. Spirit was giving me the confidence to take these exams by helping me use the information which had been in my head all my life.

I had a spirit dream, which happened at the start of my first unfoldment, when my grandmother and descendants visited me to guide me on my marriage breakdown, and to make me aware of my spiritual abilities. I can remember this spirit dream, which was 12 years ago, as if it was yesterday. It is my belief that spirit dreams are usually prophetic. Normal dreams are quickly forgotten, but spirit dreams are remembered. It is a good idea to have a notebook and pen by your bedside to make notes of anything what you consider is important in your dreams as most people can't remember their dream when they wake up.

At the time of my first unfoldment, I was aware of my close connection to my grandmother. I became aware that she was encouraging me to do things like stand in front of a large mirror to prepare me for working on the church rostrum, and she overshadowed my face with hers in a mirror. She also encouraged me to go to Sutton Church where I witnessed her communicating to me through a raised table for the first time. This is called 'table tilting'. As the table raised, I felt her energy come through. This was the strongest spirit energy I had ever felt. It was like she was standing by my side. I also was aware that she was talking to me telepathically.

Whilst trying to understand my career as a legal secretary, I could not fathom why I was never happy at work and kept moving from one firm to another. I now realise that spirit was showing me that I was capable of so much more and that is why I was unhappy.

Whilst I was on the operating table at Good Hope Hospital, undergoing a C-section giving birth, I lost a lot of blood. I believe this was another near-death experience. I remember that I was saying in my mind that I would give my life for my son, but I was subsequently told that it was not my time!

There is one significant incident that I can remember, whilst working for a large solicitors in the city whilst I was pregnant, the senior partner approached me and put his hands on my tummy and said, 'Bless you.' I believe he saw my light, just as my grandmother told me about in my spirit dream. Jacqui Rogers also referred to my light when she first saw me on the front row of a Sunday congregation at Sutton Coldfield Spiritualist Church. I also believe that people who I worked with throughout my career also saw my light, which is why my work colleagues loved me, which they subsequently came back to tell me years later.

Whilst working for a firm of solicitors in Sutton Coldfield, my manager told me to write down all my concerns. When he considered everything that I had written, he said he could see that I seemed to be doing everything for a purpose, and that something was going on, but he did not have time to go through all of it. Consequently, I had to leave this firm as I just couldn't concentrate on my work anymore as I was too focused on having a spiritual life.

Whilst visiting a coffee shop at the time of my first unfoldment, when I was struggling to cope with my psychic ability, a tramp entered the shop begging for money. When he approached me, I could feel his pain. I took my purse out of my handbag and gave him the contents, which of course he was grateful for.

During the breakdown of my marriage whilst I was still at my matrimonial home, pipes burst around the house, which could possibly have been poltergeist activity. The activity started whilst I was there, but increased with velocity after I had left. I was aware of the continuance of the plumbing issues after I left as my ex-husband had posted on Facebook what was happening whilst he was there with my son. It was obvious that the whole house was in total devastation before he left! I have included spirit guidance on understanding ghosts, which includes poltergeist activity, later in this book.

As my development progressed, I noticed that strange people came up to me for guidance in the most unusual of places. One was at the local jobcentre, when a young man sat by my side, and asked me for my opinion. I took him to a local coffee shop to talk about his issues. The man was very apologetic about having to share his problems with me. The second was in a McDonald's toilet in Birmingham where I heard a woman crying out that her man had treated her badly and she asked for my guidance. My grandmother (in spirit) had told me that I was like a candle and that strangers would be drawn to my light for guidance, and this was exactly what was happening here!

Since the time of my first unfoldment, I also became aware that spirit was sending various people to me who all seemed to be making me aware of my abilities. One incident was where an established medium put two crosses in my hands, and I made an immediate psychometric connection to his mum and dad. He said that he had never made a connection to his father before. I saw his dad as a grumpy old man, poking at his fire in desperation for it to work. I also saw his mother as a ballerina. He confirmed that everything I said was correct! So, this showed me that I had the ability of psychometry, and it again proved that my abilities were intensifying. I recognised that when I was more relaxed, my abilities were stronger.

Spirit inspired me to do a degree, the purpose of which was to improve my communication skills so that I could understand my own unfoldment, and be able to help others with theirs. I believe that spirit helped me use the information in my mind to help me fulfil a deep desire which I had within me of achieving a degree. Although spirit was trying to help me, I believe they also had their own agenda in that they wanted me to use my knowledge to help others.

Throughout the time of my development, I became aware that spirit was using my keyboard skills, which I had gained as a legal secretary, to help me communicate with the outside world which I previously had issues with.

These are just a few of the many strange occurrences that have happened to me throughout the whole of my life. When I finally believed in my messages and my visions, it became obvious to me that spirit was making me remember the whole of my life for a 'purpose' – something one of my managers had said to me in the past!

Spirit came to me only when I asked them for help with my life. They will only come to you if you ask them to, as they are not allowed to guide someone with their life unless they want them to!

16

Hearing and believing

After documenting numerous strange occurrences and spirit messages throughout my life, I could no longer deny their existence. I believe that I documented these because I needed to prove, not just for others, but also to myself what I had been experiencing over time.

One thing I was sure of was that I now realised that whenever I believed in myself, good things happened, and when I did not believe in myself, bad things happened. I also became aware that when I started to believe in my abilities, I became aware of how to use the same. However, it did take me a while to find the right teacher though! My grandmother (in spirit) had taught me the basics of mediumship, but she did not teach me everything, as there is more information available now to the world than was available in her day!

On my journey, I came across barriers such as being unable to talk about what I was experiencing because I was so scared, and when I was eventually able to talk about what had happened, I was still fearful that people would not believe me. I also came across barriers put up by other people and found it extremely difficult to find people who I trusted to get further guidance on my journey. However, as soon as I discovered Sutton Coldfield Spiritualist Church, which is connected to the Spiritualists" National Union (SNU), I knew I was in good hands. I would urge my readers that if they are ever fearful of anything in their life that they should seek the guidance of their local Spiritualist Church who have experience of spiritual matters.

Now that I have finally told the people that matter about my spiritual journey, I am now free of barriers and ready to move forward on my correct spiritual path which was always intended for me!

I sincerely hope that you discover the love of spirit and learn to believe in your Spirit Guides, as I did, so that they can guide you whenever you need their help!

17

Spirituality and spiritualism

On my journey, I learned that these two terms are often misunderstood. Although both words look alike, their meanings are very different from each other. I shall therefore examine each of them in detail.

Spirituality exists within the mind of a person. It is a condition or a state that is achieved by a person, maybe after a long period of attempts and trials e.g., yoga, acupuncture. It is a state of mind that is achieved based on a subjective experience or according to religious ideals. In similar terms, we can identify 'spirituality' in people who have attained an extreme state of mind, which is far more beyond the physical existence. This can also be identified as a process of human transformation from one psychological state to another. Many religions have identified this psychological transformation of the mind and have interpreted it in many ways. However, spirituality is not a product of religion only, but the person who should put his/her effort in achieving the state of mind or the higher level. Spirituality does not have a direct relationship with the outer appearance of the person, and he/she may remain like the same, but his/her inner self is much more advanced.

Spiritualism, however, is a belief that people may have, who call themselves spiritualists, that the spirit of a dead person can communicate with the living. The spirit comes through the medium, whoever that may be, with the desire of passing on love and encouragement. Spiritualists either communicate with spirit themselves or visit establishments where they ask mediums to allow their loved ones to come through with messages for them. They might either ask for a private reading or visit a church, and within their mind ask for their loved ones to come through. There is no exact science to this. If the enquirer does not receive any messages from a medium, it might be for any number of reasons. What happens frequently is that the sitter wants a certain spirit to come through, but instead another spirit comes through, which may be because that spirit thinks he has something to say.

Spiritualists believe that, when a person dies, he/she has an afterlife and can keep in contact with the living. However, this has many interpretations in different religions. Some of the things that are commonly shared by all the believers of spiritualism include their belief that the soul of a person has an afterlife, and that there is an existence beyond the physical body of humans, even after death. These afterlife beings are usually called 'spirits' and they are believed to be able to communicate with living people. The world of spirit is not a static or a stable place, as spirits can evolve should they so wish. It is also possible for them to rebirth. Moreover, spiritualists believe that spirit provides knowledge on God and the afterlife, too. There are many followers of spiritualism around the world and many people are attracted to this religion because it does not tie them to any religious texts, like other religions.

Considering the similarities between the two terms, we can see that both have a connection with the idea of an existence that is beyond the human faculty. Also, both these terms have their own religious interpretations.

In terms of the difference, 'spiritualism' is achieved by somebody after his/her death, whereas 'spirituality' 'is a state of mind which is achieved within the human life itself.

What does Spiritualism offer as a religion?

Spiritualism is too diverse to have a universal code of beliefs. Instead, spiritualists accept a set of more wide-ranging principles'. Baker, President of the Havant Spiritualist Church says that 'Spiritualists believe in freedom of religion and freedom of worship and that you worship God in your own way. Spiritualism gives you a set of values that enables you to think about how your relationship with God should be'.

The UK and the USA have their own version of these principles surrounding the Philosophy of Spiritualism.

SNU's Seven Principles (UK)

The Spiritualists' National Union (n.d) (SNU) in the UK, bases itself on the Seven Principles, which all full members must accept.

The first of these principles relates to accepting God as the creative force in the Universe, and that they are part of the life created by God.

The second of these principles relates to human beings being members of one divine family because they are from the same creative force. It is important to understand the needs of other individuals to assist them, not only to the material necessities of their fellow creatures, but also to their spiritual needs.

The third of these principles relates to spiritualists believing that communication with departed spirits occurs and their churches provide venues where communication, through mediumship, is possible and many deceased relatives and friends take advantage of this opportunity to continue to take an interest in the welfare of the living.

The fourth of these principles refers to their belief in the continued existence of the human soul and states that matter (being part of the creative force, or energy) cannot be destroyed; it merely changes its form and that spirit as it is part of the creative force, is therefore indestructible. When we die, our spirit becomes an integral part of the Spirit World. The Spirit World interpenetrates this material world, but in a different dimension. In spirit life, we have a spirit body, which until we progress far enough, is a replica of our Earthly body. Individuals in the Spirit World remain the same individuals with the same personalities and characteristics, and only progress through their own efforts. Individual personal responsibilities do not stop at death.

The fifth principle relates to personal responsibility, and states that everyone is responsible for their wrongful thoughts and deeds. No other person or outside influence can interfere with an individual's spiritual development unless they allow them to.

The sixth principle refers to the compensation and retribution hereafter for all the good and evil deeds done on Earth. As you sow, so shall you reap. These effects of this Law operate now, and do not wait until life in the Spirit World.

The seventh and final principle refers to the external progress that is open to every human soul. Every human spirit has the power to progress in wisdom and love. The rate of progress is directly proportional to the desire for mental and spiritual understanding. Each spirit can reform and deal with the wrong things it has done in the past

The National Association of Spiritualist Churches (USA) – Nine Principles

The National Association of Spiritualist Churches (2016-2022) (USA) has nine principles, which provide more information about spiritualist beliefs. They believe in infinite intelligence, that the phenomena of nature, both physical and spiritual, are the expression of infinite intelligence. They affirm that a correct understanding of such expression and living in accordance therewith, constitute true religion. They affirm that the existence and personal identity of the individual continue after the change called death. They affirm that communication with the so-called dead is a fact, scientifically proven by the phenomena of spiritualism. They believe that the highest morality is contained in the Golden Rule: 'Do unto others as you would have them do unto you'. They affirm the moral responsibility of individuals, and that we make our own happiness or unhappiness as we obey or disobey nature's physical and spiritual laws.

They affirm that the doorway to reformation is never closed against any soul here or hereafter. They affirm that the precepts of prophecy and healing are divine attributes proven through mediumship.

Spiritualism, in essence, encourages people to discover their own spiritual journey based on certain principles. It does not tie anyone down to any creeds or dogmas which many religions have. I believe that it is for this reason that many people are branching away from traditional religions that tie them to religious texts. This is what attracted me to spiritualism because it encourages you to consider your own spiritual path based around certain principles and is not tied down to any religious texts.

18

Spiritual development

When considering your own spiritual development beyond the physical existence, you cannot go far wrong by considering the words of mystics.

Sadhguru (2012) is dedicated to the physical, mental, and spiritual well-being of humanity. He possesses a perspective on life and living that never fails to intrigue, challenge, and surprise all he encounters. He regularly gives spiritual guidance on YouTube and one of these is 'Dimension Beyond the Physical' where he talks about development beyond our five senses.

In this YouTube clip, he talks about our physical body which has five senses which are sight, sound, smell, taste, and touch, which receives sensory information using these senses. To experience a dimension beyond the physical body, a perception beyond these senses must be developed or opened. These five senses work naturally for one's survival, and to go beyond these five senses we must strive to go beyond this barrier and develop perception beyond these senses. Your five senses naturally open the moment you leave your mother's womb because they are needed for survival. If you did not have them, you would not know how to survive. An example is where a child who is lost in the jungle who has found something edible to eat. They would naturally know to put it in their mouth. Nobody taught them this. Nobody instructed them on the way to eat. The natural skills such as eating, and walking are necessary for your survival, and you do not need any training as they are inbuilt. These inbuilt skills which are needed for survival open naturally without any striving.

There are other abilities that you are not aware of until you strive to achieve which include the abilities of being able to read and write. The way of developing perception beyond your 5 senses is known as "opening up" or "unfoldment".

All your sense organs are outward bound, you can see what is around you, but everything that you "experience" happens within you. You hear and see within you. You can see the whole world within you. An example is when you touch your friend's hand, you don't feel his hand, you can only feel your sensations on your hand. Everything that has happened to you, your joy and misery are within you – everything happens within you.

To develop your inner self and to look within you, you need to strive to achieve. Everything that we have is outward bound, but everything that is happening is within, so it gives you a false perception of what it is.

To experience anything within you, you will have to strive for and develop. turning within ourselves, but this will require development training.

"Spiritual development" is development beyond man's normal five senses which can be achieved by becoming more aware of yourself inwardly and of your surroundings. It is important to become aware of your own spiritual path to understand your development.

I conclude by saying that if you wish to develop beyond your five senses, the first step is to read spiritual books and attend circles and workshops at your local Spiritualist Church. You will discover that by mixing with likeminded people at such events you will be free to discuss any concerns that you might have in your development, and this will also help your understanding. Developing is individual and subjective, that is why it is important to discuss your journey with like-minded people who have had similar experiences.

19

Near-death experiences

To consider near death experiences, it is necessary to consider the similarities between accounts of various people. I will let spirit have the last word in this chapter by considering some of the messages from spirit which came through the mediumship of Leslie Flint (deceased).

There are many accounts of people from many different types of background around the world who have had 'near-death' experiences. We will now consider the account of a doctor who returned from a 'near-death' experience.

100huntley (2020) Dr Mark McDonough attended an interview, which was aired on YouTube on the 20th of April 2020. He wanted to share his 'near-death' experience to inspire others who had gone through similar tragedies. Unfortunately, he had suffered the tragedy of losing his mother and brother to a fire, where he tried to save them, but to no avail. At this time, he suffered multiple burns, and the pain he was suffering was so great that he asked God to take him. In his journey of recovery, he had to undergo multiple surgeries. He claims that the pain which he was experiencing was intense, but on seeing a white light he felt an awareness of 'love', his pain turned into a feeling of euphoria which took his pain away. During this surgery, he also claims that he was aware of being awake (even though he was not) and seeing his deceased relatives. He talks of a meeting between certain people, but he was not sure who they were. He was also told that it was not his time, and that he should return. Following on from this, he had more surgeries and was subsequently inspired by another doctor, whom he held in high regard. This doctor encouraged him to return to medical school to train as a trauma reconstructive surgeon. He says that he is sharing his story as he now wants to pass onto others the inspiration that he received at a difficult time of his life.

In considering the subjective accounts of various people, it is important to consider the similarities between them, despite their many and varied backgrounds. Similarities between these accounts include:

- Ability to know what is happening, not only around them, but beyond the room where they are – hearing/seeing/feeling their surroundings.
- Seeing a white light.
- Feeling unconditional love which took away their fear.
- Their pain leaves them, leaving them feeling euphoric.
- Feeling of becoming separate from their body.
- Feeling that they no longer must prove anything.
- Feeling of being loved, just because of their existence.
- Some are given the chance to remain in spirit or to return to Earth. If they choose to remain in

spirit, they will be shown what effect this will have on their family.

- If they are encouraged to return from their near-death experience, they are given the message to return and to live life fearlessly!
- Meeting relatives.
- Acknowledging separability from everything else.
- Experiencing being in a realm where they do not feel tied by talking, as they feel the essence of people that are with them, communicating with their mind. They understand the situation they are in without talking. This suggests telepathic communication with spirits, which is what I have experienced myself.

In considering the many messages that came through Leslie Flint (medium) during his lifetime, they all have a similar message to pass on: they do not want us to fear death any longer. In their words, 'there is no death, you return to a spiritual existence'. In their many messages, they all claim to give us hope that there is survival after death, they talk about many things including what they experienced when they first entered the Spirit World. They talk about people retaining the same appearance and characteristics. They talk about life in the Spirit World. They talk about understanding the lower and higher realms, and their wish to inspire people that progression is available for all that seek it!

In conclusion, only subjective proof is available about life after death until science branches away from their requirement of 100% objective proof. However, one advancement that has been made by the medical profession is that they are now accepting a more holistic approach in treating physical illnesses, and now recognise inner conflicts and disharmonies as being the cause of many troubles which do not yield to normal physical medications. For this reason, it is now accepted by medical science that the human organism should be approached and treated with a far wider concept of its constitution. This is a significant breakthrough which means that the medical profession is now more tolerant of the connection between our physical and spiritual bodies which gives hope for their future acceptance of life after death!

20

The afterlife

The afterlife, also referred to as 'life after death' or 'the world to come', is a purported existence in which the essential part of an individual's identity, or their stream of consciousness, continues to live after the death of their physical body. We will now consider whether death is the end of consciousness or whether consciousness continues after death.

For spiritual people to consider that death is the end, is short-sighted. For scientists and the medical world to consider life after death without objective proof is an impossibility - until spirit convinces them, that is!

We will now consider various countries' beliefs on 'the continuous of the soul after death'. Many worldwide authors write about a trend towards people beginning to withdraw from certain religions and considering other directions such as 'spiritualism', due to them not wanting to be fearful of life after death anymore.

The five great world religions are Judaism, Christianity, Islam, Buddhism, and Hinduism, which all have their own unique sacred texts, and all believe in some version of a 'self', which mostly survives death.

Agnostics think that it is impossible to know whether there is a God or life after death.

Atheists believe that there is no God, and no life after death, and that death is the cessation of the existence of the individual.

Despite not believing in 'life after death', Agnostics and Atheists have reported having near-death experiences.

To consider what Atheists believe regarding life after death, we will now contemplate an excerpt from YouTube by NourFoundation (2014) discussing 'Experiencing Death: An Insider's Perspective'. It focuses on the near-death experiences of Atheists and considers how much our prior beliefs shape our experiences. By considering two case studies, they question why Atheists have near-death experiences if they don't believe in angelic beings. The conclusion that they come to is: 'Just believing you don't believe anything is going to happen, does not stop it happening'. The first case that they consider is that of a lady who was careful in her interpretation, but claimed that she 'dissolved into pure energy, and when she reached the light, she had an overwhelming experience of love'. The other case study involved someone who claimed they saw dead relatives, which is common in near-death experiences. The final decision that they came to was that 'just because you do not believe that something is going to happen does not stop it happening'.

Other religions that do believe in life after death base their belief on teachings in their scriptures or traditions. But the religion of spiritualism not only believes in life after death, they also regularly demonstrate this by allowing spirits to come through mediums with messages from the afterlife.

Since the beginning of the internet, people have been searching for answers regarding whether there is an 'after life'. We will now consider a scientific view.

Farafan, A. (2017) claims that they can 'prove' that the soul does not 'DIE: It returns to the UNIVERSE'. This article was written by two scientists who question and tackle the age-old question: 'Is there life after death?' Their theory is that when we die, the contents of 'microtubules' (as they call them) return to the universe. Although this account is interesting, it is clearly written by scientists, who only believe in science. They do not even consider that there may be spiritual answers to explain 'life after death', which appears to be short-sighted considering the many accounts available to the contrary.

Let's just say that their assumption of the human soul dissipating into the universe is true. How then can thousands of mediums be getting messages from different spirits, if a person's consciousness is 'dissipating' to a universal memory where everyone's energy becomes one? This just doesn't make sense! Remember, there are many mediums all over the world who truly believe they are connecting with the Spirit World, and we owe it to them to consider their opinions when considering whether there is 'life after death'.

Even the film world has embraced the World of Spirit by depicting people having contact with the Spirit World. Examples of these films include the *Sixth Sense*, *Beetlejuice*, *What Dreams May Come*, and *Ghost*, to name but a few.

We will now consider Spirit's last word on life after death. After listening to many accounts of The Leslie Flint Trust (1997-2022), spirits come back with their love and with the aim of proving the continuous existence of the human soul after death. They come to tell us what a beautiful, magical place the Spirit World is and how we keep the same characteristics that we have on Earth. They also tell us that it is up to us whether we wish to progress to higher realms where we no longer need to be recognised as we were on Earth. 'You are not in a dark room forever; it is the start of a great journey!'

21

Spirit speaks through me

The following messages were sent by spirit through me, the first whilst I was in a trance state and the second whilst I was in a conscious state, whilst using a typewriter.

Coping with loneliness

The following message came through me to help a lady who was suffering with loneliness.

I attended a trance lesson at Arthur Findlay College on 4th October 2021, at which I was invited to connect to fellow students and practise trance mediumship. I connected to a German lady, who witnessed my trance state and made the following comments after. She talked about how my message touched her as it gave her solace as to her loneliness. This was the first time that I had experienced induced trance mediumship.

She said that when I started, she could see a flickering of my eyes. There was something behind me. It seemed to her like a halo. She could also see some heat when I connected. She could see it rather than feel it. There was a strong palpitation of my heat. Before and later, it slowed down. There was a nice and strong energy around me. The blending was wonderful. It was a perfect match. She said that my message really touched her because what I talked about was also her topic, when the world would come together as one.

The following are my words which attracted and touched her most:

'...Many people have many different thoughts. Many people only listen to their own thoughts. The understanding is not always easy. When there is understanding, there is happiness and no sadness. We should realise that we are not alone. They send love to us and words that are needed. When we are all aware, people will understand. The knowledge comes down to everyone who is ready to receive the knowledge. Some people may question spirit intelligence, but the knowledge only comes to those that are ready for it. Ask, and the true meaning of love will come to us, and then everyone will be together as one. We will be one voice, no separation of language. We will understand each other. When people work together and stand together, they will not stand apart, and everyone will share the love. Stop and listen. Stop and share.'

The German lady said that what touched her the most was when I was referring to 'loneliness', as that was what she was experiencing at the time. She enjoyed hearing about the love that was there – the oneness and togetherness.

Coping with the loss of a loved one

The following spirit message was sent to help people cope with the loss of a loved one. I was fully conscious, using a typewriter, when this message came through me.

Spirit wants to speak to you

I am trying to speak to you.
I am trying to share my love.
I am trying to share my memories.
You think you cannot hear me, but you can.
My words will not be words like you are used to,
they will be like the sounds of a rustling tree,
so listen carefully.
At first, my words will seem just like sounds, but
relax and you will understand my message to you.
You think that I am far away,
but I am closer than you think.
I am but a thought away whenever
you need my support.
You wish you had said certain words
to me before I passed.
Don't worry, I heard you speak those
words to me in your thoughts.
I now feel what you felt, and see what you have
seen, and what you see now.
I am here for you. I am Spirit. We are both Spirit.

I never know when spirit is going to send the next message. On a few occasions they have woken me up in the middle of the night when I can feel them drawing me to the keyboard. The feeling is so intense, they fill my mind with so much love it is hard not to do as they wish. All they wish to do is to share their love with the world. All they wish to do is to help us not to be so scared of death and to value our time on the Earth plane and to learn about our spiritual journey, which is to not only to look after ourselves, but to look after each other, physically and spiritually.

22

Spirit speaks on ghosts

Harry Price (deceased) on 'Ghosts', courtesy of The Leslie Flint Trust (1997-2022)

Leslie Flint was a very powerful physical medium whose lifetime spanned from 1911 to 1994. His mediumship was unique because he connected to spirit via a voice box, which appeared above his head, through which spirit spoke.

The following is an account of a spirit message which came through Leslie from Harry Price, the well-known British psychical researcher and author, who passed away in 1948. Harry Price is best remembered for his investigations into the haunting of Borley Rectory in Essex. On 19th December 1963, Harry gave a detailed account, through Leslie, explaining the difference between ghosts and spirit.

This message is one of many that comes from Leslie's archives, which are now maintained by The Leslie Flint Trust (1997-2022). The following transcript of the recording of Harry Price is produced with their kind permission. In this recording, Harry Price talks about ghosts, which he studied when he was alive. He said that spirit believed mankind needed guidance on this subject. You will notice that, as this is a message from Harry Price, it is in the first person.

Transcript

Harry Price: Now I am on the other side; I realise how difficult it is to prove anything appertaining to psychic matters in a purely material or scientific way. We must accept the fact that scientific proof – that is the kind of proof that would appeal and would be accepted, strictly on scientific grounds or scientific basis by scientific minds – is practically impossible to prove 100%. It may to some extent accept with reservations, but science is too anxious for 100% proof on a scientific basis of something which I feel cannot be accepted scientifically or proved scientifically. I come to give a talk on ghosts to answer certain problems about them.

Often one hears of ghosts and entities that haunt a certain place, often for centuries, and sometimes they are, according to the mentality of the ghosts in question, a nuisance and sometimes they are very much undesirable from the point of view that they disturb and frighten individuals who happen to be living on the premises. Firstly, I should differentiate because there are varying kinds of ghosts.

First, you have the ghost of an individual, perhaps long since dead, that has no connection with the actual spirit of the person concerned. You may have a very powerful thought force which may, by its very power, give the impression that the individual person or personality is there at the haunting. There are a lot of people, when they have seen what they term to be a ghost, are under the impression that they are seeing the apparition in outward shape and form of the individual who has long since been dead. What is happening there is that the individual concerned is not necessarily present. This is an astral projection upon the atmosphere which on certain occasions (usually because the atmosphere is conducive to it) manifests itself in shape or appearance. But this apparition has no power whatsoever because the mentality or the mind of the individual – the ghost – is not there, is not present. In other words, it is a kind of a shell that is formed out of the ether under certain given conditions, quite often at certain times, and it has a limited power. It can only move in certain areas and under certain conditions and can only be seen, quite often, by people who are (without realising it) mediumistic or sensitive to the extent that they can see onto that vibration which is all around the Earth – which is very much used, often by spiritualist mediums, to link up and to tune in with spirits from other spheres. By this, I am trying to convey that a ghost is an entirely different thing to a spirit. You might say a 'ghost', which has no real substance and no real power, is a very strong thought vibration which has impregnated itself upon the atmosphere in a certain given place, invariably because at the time of the death of the individual, their thoughts were so strong and powerful that they left behind a memory condition which can be to some extent tangible, although the individual concerned has recently, or at some time when the happening of the passing took place, long since left.

With a lot of these hauntings, the poltergeist has no connection with the individual. It is a condition of the past which has registered itself very strongly upon the atmosphere, thereby being able to recreate in a given form, shape, and substance of a kind which has no actual physical power – material power – but merely an etheric condition, and cannot under any circumstances do any harm whatsoever to any living person; cannot in any way do anything or say anything or have any power upon any individual that may be conscious of its presence. You may find that in very old houses, castles and so on, that these apparitions do appear, and not necessarily are they alone. For instance, there are places where great battles have been fought, where sudden death has taken place *en masse,* and the thought-force has been so powerful, so much registered around and about that spot, that there are occasions when visually that battle can be seen again. In fact, the astral or the etheric world which intermingles with yours is in a sense a mirror. It registers and can show all manner of incidences appertaining to man's life, particularly the point of death. The Earth world is surrounded, completely and absolutely, by this etheric condition of life or substance, such as it is, which contains reflections of past events. In fact, one might say that everything that has happened of any consequence, individually and collectively to man, is still in the atmosphere.

Even the most ordinary of people may go to a house with the intent to buy that house or to live in that house in the future, and yet not necessarily be psychic, as is generally understood in the term 'mediumship', and on opening the door will sense and feel an atmosphere. Sometimes it is so strong that no matter how pleasant the house may seem and be in many respects, they would not buy it; neither would you have it as a gift, because in that house is a power of a kind which is so strong, so powerful, that no individual would feel happy. The walls are impregnated with the thought forces of individuals, or an individual, who has lived in that place.

It is perfectly true that we ourselves create our own atmosphere and that we are all individuals, and some much more powerful than others; and regarding our possessions when on Earth, our houses, our places of worship, and so on, you will find varying conditions. Usually, they are quite pleasant and liveable. But there are these places where deeds have taken place, things have happened to individuals which have so impregnated the very walls, and the atmosphere – even though the spirit has gone on in the spheres – has been left behind, which registers to such an extent that no-one feels disposed to live in those vibrations and conditions.

Unfortunately, the Spirit World knows so little about vibrations. Vibrations are always being quoted regarding séances. He says that he believes that science in our world today is gradually discovering much more about vibration: what it can achieve, what it can do, what it is. But even so there's a limit, I feel, to what science may discover about psychic forces; because psychic forces are, in themselves, unscientific from the material point of view. They are so powerful, too, and they cannot necessarily be harnessed in a material sense.

A house that retains powerful vibrations of thought forces is not easily altered or changed. Quite often it's a common thing when a house is reputed to be haunted to call in, perhaps, a local clergyman or canon or a dean or someone to exorcise. There is no such thing as being able to exorcise a power which manifests itself in etheric conditions unless the individual spirit is present. The only way it seems to me that a change can be brought about is not by exorcism but by the power of the individuals concerned, who may live in that building, to concentrate their thoughts in such a way that those thoughts will counteract the vibrations in and around the building; that they may release, as it were, those memory forces, those forces which in themselves have no substance but are purely mental conditions left behind by the entity that has gone ahead. In other words, by the power of thought you can change the vibrations of that building and clear it of its force, which may not necessarily be evil.

Regarding evil influences or evil spirits, it is very rare indeed that you have a place that is evil (if you accept evil in the sense that it is generally accepted). Individual forces from individual minds create certain conditions which are not always easy to change, easy to alter, but it can be done when you understand more about this subject of haunting. The etheric, the substance, and it is a substance, in which is registered all manner of things appertaining to the past, cannot necessarily be changed but it can be so affected by thought forces from your side, from your world, right thought forces of good, to counteract and disperse something which is unpleasant and unnecessary.

There is a vast difference between these so-called apparitions which have no real power than, for instance, to a haunting which is of an individual spirit. And where you have the individual spirit haunting a place or staying around a place or appearing at certain times in a place, that – because it has real substance behind it: the thought force and the power of that thought of the individual – is an entirely different matter altogether.

And it is possible to communicate with that spirit by mind and ask that spirit to leave and to help that spirit; because invariably they need help: they're Earth-bound and you can help them.

At 'Borley' the Rectory that was, and in the church itself, where there was a manifestation which was very real, was not of one person but of two. One was of a nun who for many years had clung to the place. She had been very ill-treated and had been seduced and her child had been destroyed in infancy and to keep her quiet she had been murdered; and, of a monk who was responsible. This happened many centuries ago and you would have thought that a soul would have, over many centuries, long since departed. This nun appeared at intervals, and she was anxious – one would have thought after so long a time that it would have been rather pointless – but nevertheless she was anxious for the skeleton, the body, to be discovered and of the child.

The monk himself committed suicide later that was hushed up. This is going back many centuries – somewhere round about nearly 400 years. Here there was no evil; there was nothing there which could be considered unpleasant. It was simply that from time to time she was drawn back to Earth by thought forces and memories of past events and of the desire for justice to be done, and this strange idea, too, for the body to have been buried in hallowed ground, which was then considered very important. Since she herself was not buried in hallowed ground, it held her in some sense closer to Earth. She wanted to see this brought into being, this justice being done; but this is only one isolated case.

There are thousands of authenticated cases of individuals who have seen manifestations sometimes of the individual concerned who is troubled in their mind and wants some matter put right that was left undone, or someone brought to justice for some deed that had been done against them, such as murder. Most of these cases are well authenticated, were individuals who were perturbed in their minds and could not find peace and rest and haunted certain places with a hope of either bringing justice into being regarding themselves, or to perhaps show where money had been hidden which preyed on their mind after death, or for some reason such as that.

But there is a vast difference between these individual hauntings by individual spirits than there is to these other apparitions that have no substance as such, which are merely etheric manifestations in the ether of thought forces long since, as far as the individual person's concerned, long since departed. Particularly in places like the Tower of London there are these etheric forces hovering around the building. It has also been well authenticated with individual soldiers, for instance, on duty who've seen apparitions without any shadow of a doubt – but they're not necessarily the individuals: they are thought force creations in the ether which at certain given times, under certain given conditions, can be seen, can be even spoken to. It is very rare that a ghost speaks. They have not the power of speech. But where you have an individual – that is an entity – who returns to Earth, they are sometimes able to register sound waves or to vibrate sound waves and make themselves heard, and they are audible.

Poltergeists are invariably individuals who are Earth-bound who do, by the power which they may have under the conditions which they exist in the place, are able to use various things to attract attention. Usually, you'll find there is someone in that household – quite often a young person –– who's full of vitality and power and psychic force, makes it possible for them to become more material in as much that they can either if they cannot be seen, they can use the power drawn from the individual in the household to move furniture or to throw things about. This is a deliberate attempt at communication; invariably not spiteful, very rarely spiteful, usually done in exasperation to attract attention to themselves, invariably because they wish something in that house to be discovered. It may be money that is hidden, or it could be, perhaps, even a body that has been buried, perhaps under the floorboards. There are many reasons and very good reasons why some spirits do return and haunt places, because they want something put right that is disturbing them. They cannot, as it were, rest or settle in their new environment; they are concerned with material things because those material things are very much on their mind. They realise that there's something that they want to put right and until it's put right, they do not feel they can leave the Earth world – they cannot leave without this matter being settled. I will give an example of a person that will die leaving money hidden perhaps in floorboards or something, and it worries them. They feel that they should have left a Will or indicated where this money was hidden and so on.

All manner of things causes people to be Earth-bound and this is not necessarily a long-lasting thing. Usually, a person is not Earth-bound for a very long time because after a time, if they are not able to get in touch, eventually they begin to realise the futility of trying to do something in a material sense (which often they realise is impossible) to attract the attention sufficiently to make it possible for what it is they wish to convey to be understood, and they leave. But you do get the persistent types who will cling and will hold on and they will in consequence do everything in their power, particularly if they feel within themselves, it's essential that it should be attended to or done. Examples include the apparitions of horses, of dogs, of cats, even of birds: now these apparitions are not necessarily real from the point of view that the soul is present. Invariably these come under the category of etheric manifestations which are thought-force on the ether which at certain times is visible. These phantom horse-drawn carriages: they have no real substance. But there is a kind of reality in as much that they are seen and witnessed by people on your side, but they have no real substance. In fact, they are etheric reproductions of events that have taken place, perhaps hundreds of years ago which are very strong and powerful and continue to register, often for many years

There are some very amusing ghosts: ghosts with a great sense of humour. Sometimes, you do get individuals who have a wonderful sense of humour, and they do from this side endeavour to do things which cause perhaps some irritation or annoyance, but there is a sense of fun; because we on this side, as you know, are not necessarily changed immediately by death. We are very much the same people – that's one thing that I've discovered since I've been here, that this is a world of reality.

Our world is a world of illusion in as much that so much that goes on, that you accept as factual and real, to them is very unreal apart from being factual. This is the world of reality, and we have the attributes, and we have the defects often that we may have had on Earth. *(He made a joke about those spirits don't suddenly become angels and that they see the funny side sometimes of the goings on in our world, particularly with individuals that we're fond of.)* At certain times people come back from their side and they enter your life, take an interest in what you're doing and, of course, they can see more deeply than people on your side can see, into the hearts and minds of others. And they do see things which possibly the individual concerned endeavours to hide very carefully from others, very successfully, but we see the full person. They don't see just a façade and don't see what people would like others to see and ignore the rest. They see everything with a sense of fun. Sometimes individuals from their side, who are by no means bad souls, do things to try and jerk people in your world out of themselves, to make them conscious of things which are more important, and to make them think and act differently in their own personal lives.

There is a reason and a purpose of hauntings on their side. Sometimes it strikes them as rather funny when a clergyman starts to try and exorcise because no-one has the power to exorcise. I am quite sure the average clergyman hasn't a clue about this whole subject. In fact, clergymen do not have the vaguest notions about communication, about spirits. The average church man is very ignorant of the truths of life after death and has a vague belief which may be to him a reality, but there is no substance behind it to prove my statements. They come often to jerk out of themselves these very people who would exorcise us. Sometimes a haunting that may take place is deliberate in as much that it may bring in the clergyman and make him try to do something about it; but much more important to make him think more seriously about it – make him think more seriously about the possibilities of life after death and communication; to try and make him know there is something in the truth of survival.

A lot of things that go on which sometimes seem a little bewildering are done deliberately by our side. The apparitions that one sees occasionally as mentioned may be etheric remembrances of things past registered upon the atmosphere with no deep substance or reality of individual life. But a lot of the individual hauntings by spirits – apart from those who come because they wish to have something put right – a lot of it is done by souls from this side with the deliberate intention of arousing interest at certain times and at certain places to bring all manner of people to the realisation that there is something outside of your normal so-called existence. And if we can bring the church into it, who preach so much about life after death, and make them think more seriously about it, and the possibility of communication as well, then we're doing a jolly good job.

Spirit uses all manner of methods, all manner of ways, for trying to bring realisation and truth of survival to the world, and hauntings are quite often something which to us is a method and a way of arousing interest. And if we can get the local clergyman, or the canon or whoever he may be, into the house, or into the place, and get a lot of newspaper publicity about it, then we are setting people thinking and wondering, and also the parson himself (if it's possible to make him realise that he is also being used as a medium) making him think about survival and communication, we're on the right track of infiltrating truth in all directions. So, there are many reasons for this.

There are cases of individuals who are Earth-bound because of ignorance and because they're held so much down by material thoughts within themselves. They are materialists in life that they cannot fail to be – although in a sense apart from the Earth – materialists still, and they cling to those things they know and those conditions that they like, and for a time they live in a kind of illusionary world. They seem to have pleasure and fun and happiness of a kind out of making other people do the kind of things that they like doing. In other words, of course, they sometimes impinge themselves on individuals in your world and use them often for their own ends and that, of course, is bad and could in some instances be dangerous.

There are all manner and forms and conditions appertaining to hauntings, appertaining to apparitions and spirits. Spirit wants very much to give a much clearer picture of this because it is a very important thing for people on your side to know about.

Sitter: Why do places go cold when a spirit's presence is felt?

Harry Price: I do not know. I guess in the process of drawing energy and power from, perhaps, individuals on our side make the manifestation possible that they may be taking something from the atmosphere which gives warmth. This is a feasible solution. There is always this and I have experienced it when on our side... of the coldness and the feeling as if there is something not normal or natural. But this may be due to a mental thing more than a physical – it may be a mental process which has a physical reaction, and the coldness is the reaction that you have. It may not be that the temperature changes; it may be an illusionary thing of change in temperature. Although it has been ascertained, I believe, by a so-called scientific method of noting that the atmosphere has dropped, and the temperature has dropped. As I have already said, there are these Earth-bound souls who cling to individuals and use those individuals and often detrimentally.

Sitter: Do you know anything about the famous scientist, Sir William Crookes.

Harry Price: I don't know very much about this, but I have heard certain things said about him that weren't very complimentary. There will always be those who will, if they can by one means or other... some means or other... they'll use foul means to blacken the name of a person who has done so much to progress science and truth. It is the best thing to ignore these things because they will be accepted by the kind of mentalities that want to accept and discarded by those who are not of the same mentality. It's a problem. There is an old Chinese proverb: 'the tall trees gather the most wind'. I think that's perfectly true. The higher you become or the more famous you are, the more you become an 'Aunt Sally'. Do not worry too much about it because truth will out eventually. Regarding any criticism of a moral nature which I believe was suggested regarding Crookes, I think that one can ignore that; and that he would be party to something which was, well, fraudulent is ridiculous. He wouldn't risk and stake his reputation on something of that nature. A man who's got so much to lose – a good name – would not be party to anything, unless it was completely honest and straightforward. It is stupid that an intelligent person would refute and disagree with such a ghastly thing.

The author's experience of Poltergeists

I believe that I have experienced the power of a poltergeist where, during my marriage break-up, there were widespread plumbing issues through my matrimonial home. I believe that a poltergeist could have used the bad psychic energy between my ex-husband and myself to cause havoc, which I believe devalued our house. I have asked a world-class medium about this issue, and she agreed with me that it sounded like a poltergeist experience.

Final word

Now that I have relayed an account of my spiritual journey, I am in a better place to move forwards to help others with their spiritual journey.

When searching for knowledge to help you understand your spiritual journey, it is important to listen to your inner messages and be vigilant as to what is happening around you, as spirit might be trying to bring your attention something that is relevant to your journey!

My final words are 'BELIEVE AND YOU WILL ACHIEVE', as it was only when I started to believe in my own spiritual pathway that I achieved the spiritual path which was always meant for me!

Wendy Sheffield

References

100huntley (2020) (Doctor has near-death experience that transforms his life)
https://www.youtube.com/watch?v=sv0ZPnXU-9E
Viewed: 2nd May 2022

Arthur Findlay College (2018) (Psychic and Mediumship course)
https://www.arthurfindlaycollege.org
Viewed: 16th May 2022

Baker, A. (President of the Havant Spiritualist Church)

Beetlejuice (1988) (Film)

Bible, The: Acts 2:4

Eckhart, T (2020) (The Beginning of Awakening and Essential Identity)
https://www.youtube.com/watch?v=S_o2iOavxYI
Viewed: 15th April 2022

Farafan, A. (2017) THE UNEXPLAINED Scientists 'prove' that the soul does not DIE: It returns to the UNIVERSE'

https://www.linkedin.com/pulse/unexplained-scientists-prove-soul-does-die-returns-universe-تارات
Viewed: 15.4.2022

Ghost (1990) (Film)

Kelford, J. and Beech, C. International Mediums

Leslie Flint Trust, The (1997-2022) (Harry Price)
https://leslieflint.com/harry-price
Viewed :15.4.2022

National Spiritualist Association of Churches (2016-2022) (9 Principles)
https://nsac.org/
Viewed: 25th May 2022

NourFoundation (2014) (Do |Atheists have Near-Death Experiences?) The New York Academy of Sciences
https://www.youtube.com/watch?v=rUfW_Ek54sA
Viewed: 1st May 2022

Rogers, J. (Medium and Author of *Simply Spiritual)*

Sadhguru (2012) (Dimension Beyond the Physical)
https://www.youtube.com/watch?v=WJWXf2A0Nb4&t=1s
Viewed: 16th May 2022

Sixth Sense, The (1999) (Film)

Spiritualists' National Union (n.d) The (Seven Principles of Spiritualism)

https://www.snu.org.uk/7-principles
Viewed :15.4.2022

Spiritualists' National Union (n.d) (SH1 Accreditation Level Course)

Sutton Coldfield Spiritualist Church, Kenelm Rd, Sutton Coldfield, B73 6HD
Phone: 0121 354 3266

What Dreams May Come (1998) (Film)

Wilson, L. (formerly of Erdington Christian Spiritualist Church)
Phone: 0121 354 3266

Lightning Source UK Ltd.
Milton Keynes UK
UKHW022148011022
409690UK00008B/95

9 781803 812038